52 *more* scrapbooking challenges

by Elizabeth Kartchner

I dare you!

Do you remember that scene in the classic movie *A Christmas Story?* The one where Flick sticks his tongue to a frozen flagpole, all because Schwartz "triple-dog dared" him, only to find himself stuck in an awkward and painful position? It's a hilarious scene that any viewer, young or old, can relate to in some way.

What is it about being "dared" to do something that gives us the courage to try new (and sometimes crazy) things? There's just something about the challenge that ups the excitement and energy, which is why I'm completely energized by this book. It dares me to take my regular scrapbooking routine and mix it up with dozens of creativity challenges. I've never been one to back down from a challenge, especially when it sounds like fun and gets my creative wheels turnin'.

What about you? Are you up for the challenge? If so, I double-dog dare you to turn to any page in this book and see what Elizabeth Kartchner and nine of her creative friends have in store. They've put together 52 fresh scrapbooking challenges for you to try. No worries—they're all completely safe and oh, so fun. No stuck tongues, just beautiful layouts and a new way to approach your scrapbooking.

Ready to give it a try? Come on, I triple-dog dare you!

Megan Hoeppner

MEGAN HOEPPNER CREATIVE EDITOR

P.S. To create this page, I took on challenge 13 on p. 46 and added a single color to an otherwise black-and-white page. My wedding colors were black, ivory and red, so I modified this challenge to use black and ivory with color to fit my theme. Using this palette is a great way to simplify the creative process and make a statement with color.

Flower Girls *by Megan Hoeppner.* **Supplies** *Patterned paper:* Chatterbox, Doodlebug Design and Heidi Grace Designs; *Letter stickers:* American Crafts and Chatterbox; *Journaling spot:* Close To My Heart; *Pen:* American Crafts; *Adhesive:* Scrapbook Adhesive by 3L; *Other:* Ribbon.

Free yourself

It's fascinating—the deeper I dig into stuff my mom saved from my childhood, the more I realize that I've been scrapbooking practically my whole life. One of my favorite projects is from my 5th grade camp, where I cut letters straight from a photo of the mountains for a title and saved bits and pieces of my adventure to include in the album.

There's no doubt that the reasons I fell in love with scrapbooking then are the same reasons I love this hobby today. Knowing that behind the photos there are stories longing to be told, to be savored and it's up to us to do it—I take that very seriously. Whether it's the silly things my child says, eating pancakes for an afternoon snack or cherishing a relationship, I feel a deep yearning to not let moments become lost, but celebrated and retold with each turn of the page.

Looking back at my early, prized pages, I also recognize that I have always enjoyed challenging myself when I sit down to create. Whether it's in my design, photos or a cool technique, I strive to try something new and exciting with each page. So you could imagine my excitement when *Creating Keepsakes* magazine asked me to be the author for a second volume of scrapbooking challenges (the first was published in 2006). After I came down from dancing on the moon, there was a creative journey ahead of me to fill this book with fun challenges and inspiring layouts.

First we came up with 52 challenges, then chose some talented girls to contribute astounding pages. Next came writing, photography and design . . . and here we are with a fabulous book overflowing with techniques, quizzes and step-by-step instructions.

As you hold this book I hope you are enthused—I picture you sitting down to create, thrilled to let go of expectations and ready to have fun! Stretching ourselves creatively is freeing, and in the end it brings us closer to finding our authentic scrapbooking style.

Free yourself in your scrapbooking…

♡*lizzy*

ELIZABETH KARTCHNER

Contents

journaling

techniques

photo fun

Keepsakes

EDITOR IN CHIEF, *CREATING KEEPSAKES* BRIAN TIPPETTS
MANAGING EDITOR, SPECIAL PRODUCTS JENNAFER MARTIN
CREATIVE EDITOR MEGAN HOEPPNER
SENIOR WRITER BETH OPEL
SENIOR EDITOR LORI ANDERSON
CREATIVE DIRECTOR ERIN BAYLESS
ART DIRECTOR MARIN BARNEY
PHOTOGRAPHY BRIAN SMITH & SYMONI JOHNSON FOR BPD STUDIOS

CK MEDIA

CEO WILL MARKS
CFO RICH HYBNER
VP/GROUP PUBLISHER DAVID O'NEIL
VP/EDITORIAL DIRECTOR LIN SORENSON
VP/DIRECTOR OF EVENTS PAULA KRAEMER
SR. PRODUCTION DIRECTOR TERRY BOYER

LEISURE ARTS
the art of everyday living

EDITOR IN CHIEF SUSAN WHITE SULLIVAN
SPECIAL PROJECTS DIRECTOR SUSAN FRANTZ WILES
DIRECTOR OF DESIGNER RELATIONS DEBRA NETTLES
SR. PREPRESS DIRECTOR MARK HAWKINS
PUBLISHING SYSTEMS ADMINISTRATOR BECKY RIDDLE
PUBLISHING SYSTEMS ASSISTANTS CLINT HANSON,
JOHN ROSE & KEIJI YUMOTO

VP AND COO TOM SIEBENMORGEN
DIRECTOR OF FINANCE AND ADMINISTRATION LATICIA MULL DITTRICH
VP SALES AND MARKETING PAM STEBBINS
DIRECTOR OF SALES AND SERVICES MARGARET REINOLD
VP OPERATIONS JIM DITTRICH
COMPTROLLER, OPERATIONS ROB THIEME
RETAIL CUSTOMER SERVICE MANAGER STAN RAYNOR
PRINT PRODUCTION MANAGER FRED F. PRUSS

52 More Scrapbooking Challenges is published by Leisure Arts, Inc., 5701 Ranch Drive, Little Rock, Arkansas 72223-9633. 501-868-8800. www.leisurearts.com.
This product is manufactured under license for CK Media, LLC.—a CK Media company, publisher of *Creating Keepsakes*® scrapbook magazine. ©2009. All rights reserved.

Tippetts, Brian
Creating Keepsakes
"A Leisure Arts Publication"

ISBN-13: 978-1-57486-030-6 • ISBN-10: 1-57486-030-5

inspired by...

If you're a scrapbooker, you're creative—period. You may not always feel it. I certainly don't. But I truly believe that if we nurture our imaginations and learn how to discover and utilize inspiration, the sky's the limit! Have fun flexing your creative muscle with the challenges in this chapter.

1 Get inspired by an outfit.

I never outgrew playing dress-up—it's just too fun! For me, fashion is all about playing with patterns and colors and textures and proportion, just like scrapbooking! So for this challenge I want you to find an outfit that appeals to you, whether it's from your own closet, off a mannequin at your favorite boutique, or out of an online or print catalog. Let the shapes, color combination or patterns inspire your next page. Check out how Keisha and I interpreted the outfit at left on our layouts.

You may wonder how it's possible to translate something three-dimensional into a scrapbook page. Well, the key is to reference the pieces rather than attempt to literally re-create them. I was really inspired by the mix of textures in this ensemble. To imitate the blouse's cutwork flowers, I used a die cut to create my own lace cardstock. By layering vellum, cardstock and flowers, I replicated the feel of the inspiration look and achieved a unique texture of my own.

Blissful Love by Elizabeth Kartchner. **Supplies** *Cardstock:* Wausau; *Patterned paper:* K&Company (pattern) and My Mind's Eye (pink); *Letters:* American Crafts; *Flowers:* K&Company; *Ribbon:* SEI; *Die cut:* Sizzix; *Adhesive:* Glue Dots International and Scrapbook Adhesives by 3L; *Other:* Vellum, flower sequin rhinestones, computer font and thread.

Us *by Keisha Campbell.* **Supplies** *Cardstock:* Bazzill Basics Paper (light gray and yellow) and ColorMates (dark gray); *Patterned paper:* Making Memories; *Stamps:* Hero Arts (bold floral) and Stampin' Up! (letters); *Punches:* Dogwood (large flower), McGill (brackets and buttercup) and Stampin' Up! (scallop); *Metal clip:* Stampin' Up!; *Button:* La Mode; *Other:* Vellum, pen and ink.

Keisha took her cues from both the shapes and colors of the outfit. Her gray cardstock background echoes the color of the blouse, while the subtle floral stamping and vellum blooms imitate its appliqué collar. The shape of the journaling die cut is a clear nod to the flowers. Feel free to use your favorite outfit as a jumping-off point or as a complete design strategy.

2 Draw inspiration from media.

People ask me all the time where I get my ideas. Truthfully, I might have less to say if you asked what *doesn't* inspire me. Lately, I'm finding a lot of inspiration in books, music and film. Scrapbooking has allowed me to see and hear the world with new eyes and ears. For this challenge, look and listen for a creative boost in print or recorded media.

Completely Loves Her Doggie by Elizabeth Kartchner. **Supplies** *Cardstock:* Bazzill Basics Paper; *Patterned paper:* Daisy D's Paper Co. (flags), KI Memories (red and black dot) and Sassafras (wood); *Font:* Mia's Scribblings; *Adhesive:* Glue Dots International and Scrapbook Adhesives by 3L; *Other:* Thread and pen.

I COMPLETELY KNOW ABOUT GUINEA PIGS BY LAUREN CHILD

My daughter, Avery, adores her Charlie and Lola DVD. Her favorite episode is "I Completely Know about Guinea Pigs," so I borrowed the "completely" as well as the color scheme and the large circle design element from the cover and created this layout. Even if your daily stimulation, like mine, includes a lot of children's favorites, you can find ideas, too!

THE HOTEL CAFÉ PRESENTS WINTER SONGS

The heart shape of the tree on the cover of the Winter Songs CD immediately caught Kelly's eye. Not only is it an appealing look, but it also fit well thematically with her layout concept of fall and close friends. Did you notice that she even added some tiny hearts among the tree branches? Clever girl.

Loving the Leaves *by Kelly Purkey.* **Supplies** *Cardstock:* American Crafts and Bazzill Basics Paper; *Patterned paper:* Cosmo Cricket (yellow and wood grain) and Heidi Grace Designs (orange, green and brown dot); *Stickers and brads:* American Crafts; *Punches:* Fiskars Americas; *Font:* Marketing Script; *Other:* Thread.

3 Lift a design idea from a home-decor item.

It seems that whenever I walk the aisles of Target or flip through the pages of the latest Pottery Barn catalog, I come up with a new layout design or embellishment treatment. Pretty bits for your home are created by professional designers, so harness their skills to create pretty bits for your next page!

Wishes & Kisses by Elizabeth Kartchner. **Supplies** *Cardstock and patterned paper:* American Crafts; *Letters:* American Crafts (brown) and Making Memories (pink); *Buttons:* Making Memories; *Font:* Little Days; *Adhesive:* Glue Dots International, Scrapbook Adhesives by 3L and Liquid Glue, Close To My Heart; *Other:* thread.

This adorable rug design was just begging to be made into a scrapbook page. To mimic its quirky, imperfect vibe, I simply used a craft knife to cut the loopy accent from patterned paper and punched brown circles for the dots. Stitched-on buttons give my page some texture.

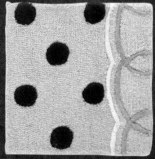

AMELIA RUG, POTTERY BARN KIDS

Fruit seems to be a recurring home-decor theme and is back in vogue these days. Cindy was really inspired by the informal brown grid pattern of the apple and pear shapes on these kitchen accessories and re-created the look on her layout with machine-stitching. Learn how on the next page!

KITCHEN LINENS:
ORLA KIELY FOR TARGET

daily

Elijah: Can I have chips for my snack?

Mommy: You can have a piece of fruit."

Elijah: But I *want* chips!

Mommy: You can have fruit, and making that sad face *won't* change my mind.

Honestly sweetie, I'd rather have chips too...but we need to eat healthy foods every day. Then we can splurge on chips every once in a while.

conversation

Daily Conversation *by Cindy Tobey.* **Supplies** *Cardstock:* Bazzill Basics Paper; *Patterned paper:* Bo-Bunny Press (green dot), Cosmo Cricket (yellow stripe) and Karen Foster Design (ruled); *Stickers:* American Crafts (brown foam letters) and Doodlebug Design (red letters); *Rub-ons:* My Mind's Eye; *Ribbon:* Cosmo Cricket; *Chipboard:* BasicGrey; *Ink:* Clearsnap; *Pen:* Sakura; *Font:* Calibri; *Other:* Thread.

Try this:

STITCH A PATTERN INSIDE A SHAPE

Cindy's textural shapes really add interest to her page. Follow these steps to re-create her technique for your next layout. It's a fabulous look!

1 Start with two layers of textured cardstock in the same color. Place the top layer texture-side up and the bottom layer smooth-side up. Cut a shape out of the top layer.

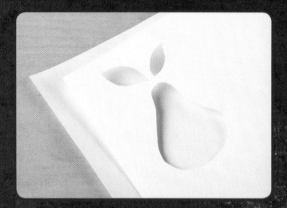

2 Machine-stitch a grid pattern with brown thread on the bottom piece of cardstock where the shape cut-out will be when you layer the papers. (You may want to lightly draw the shape outline with pencil first to be sure you sew across the entire area.)

3 Ink all the edges of the top layer and glue it, texture-side up, to the stitched shape.

4 Let a song lyric inspire a layout.

Music is such an integral part of who I am. Sometimes a song just totally pinpoints how I'm feeling or transports me back to a certain time. Incorporating song lyrics on a layout seems like a natural fit. For this challenge, both Amanda and I borrowed our layout titles from songs. What tune from your life soundtrack can you use on a page today?

LOVE IS THE SWEETEST THING BY RAY NOBLE

Love is the sweetest thing
What else on earth could ever bring
Such happiness to everything
As love's old story?

Love is the strangest thing
No song of birds upon the wing
Shall in our hearts so sweetly sing
Than love's old story.

Whatever heart may desire
Whatever fate may send
This is the song that never will tire
This is the song without end.

Love is the greatest thing
The oldest, yet the latest thing
I only hope that fate may bring
Love's story to you.

Amanda is crazy about music from the 1930s and 40s, and since this melody was running through her head, she put it to use on this charming page. Love is the main theme of both the layout and the song, so she stitched the word right onto her background. To make sure she liked the design, she sketched the word on the page first and then followed her pencil lines with the sewing machine.

Love Is the Sweetest Thing
by Amanda Johnson. **Supplies**
Patterned paper: Hambly
Screen Prints and Sassafras;
Rub-ons: Hambly Screen Prints;
Other: Notebook paper, vintage
woodgrain tape, label maker
and thread.

I admit it—sometimes I get a little stressed out when I'm taking things too seriously or putting too much pressure on myself. This song really reminds me to chill out and relax, and take time to embrace life. Now that I have this page in my album, I have a visual reminder to keep me unruffled in the face of my daily challenges. Hey—maybe I need to frame this one and put it on the wall in my craft room!

Enjoy the Show by Elizabeth Kartchner. **Supplies** *Patterned paper:* American Crafts and BasicGrey; *Transparency:* Hambly Screen Prints; *Flower clip:* KI Memories; *Ticket:* Jenni Bowlin Studio; *Glitter:* Making Memories; *Fonts:* Century Gothic and Mia's Scribblings; *Adhesive:* Glue Dots International, Scrapbook Adhesives by 3L and Liquid Glue, Close To My Heart; *Other:* Flowers, brads and spray ink.

5 Find inspiration in a print design.

Oh my gosh, there are so many cool graphic designs out there to spark your creativity. Book sleeves, product logos, billboards, posters . . . the list is endless. Go on a hunt today for an inspiring design and translate it to a scrapbooking project!

CELEBRATE STAMP,
U.S. POSTAL SERVICE

Unique by Mou Saha. **Supplies** *Cardstock:* Frances Meyer; *Patterned paper:* me & my BIG ideas (red), Rusty Pickle (yellow) and Scenic Route (green); *Stickers and corrugated letters:* Rusty Pickle; *Flower die cuts:* Die Cuts With a View; *Paint:* Making Memories, Matisse Derivan, Plaid Enterprises and Wild Iris; *Embroidery floss:* DMC; *Pen:* American Crafts; *Other:* Fabric and thread.

When Mou first spotted this postage stamp, she was inspired by both the layout of the artwork and the text treatment. Notice how she divided her cardstock into 12 equal parts, using the top six boxes to add the letters of her title and the rest for photos, accents and telling the story.

Love you love you love you!! It's easy to say but hard to communicate the extent to which my love goes! To put it simply I would do anything for you, go anywhere you go, together forever You make my world colorful, you make my eyes light up, you make my heart dance, my head spin, my belly hurt from laughing so hard. You are ♥ the jelly to my PB&J! I la la love you

la la la
LOVE
YOU

La La La Love You by Elizabeth Kartchner. **Supplies** *Cardstock:* Bazzill Basics Paper; *Patterned paper:* KI Memories and Sassafras; *Font:* Arial and Fling.

LA LA
LOVE
YOU
♥

LA LA LOVE YOU PRINT,
SPARKLEPOWER, ETSY

I'm so grateful for my husband, Collin. He just "gets" me. Sometimes I feel almost delirious about my love for him, so when I spotted this print, I just knew I wanted to nab the sentiment for a layout about him. Plus, how bold and pretty are the colors and type choices? Crop one photo two ways to make it appear like it's more than one photo and to emphasize different aspects of the picture. Though neither Mou nor I copied the original designs exactly from our inspiration pieces, you certainly can if it works for you.

Quiz:
What inspires you?

Choose your answers, then consult the key to add your totals and see how you channel your creativity.

12–15 POINTS: You're a free spirit who sees the world through colorful, beautiful lenses. Creativity comes naturally to you. You're ready to experiment and take risks and play. *Your challenge: Come up with a system to collect all your great ideas. Carry a small journal to quickly jot down thoughts or sketches when they occur to you.*

8–11 POINTS: You're an inspiration dabbler. You can make a connection between an image and your own layout goals. You seek inspiration and can easily recognize a great idea. *Your challenge: Pick up a fashion or home-decor magazine or catalog and look at it with scrapbooking in mind. Can you find a cool text treatment or page-layout idea?*

5–7 POINTS: You're ready to open your mind to inspiration. You like to have a plan and getting pages done efficiently is important to you. You may not think of yourself as very creative, but you are! You just like to be creative within a plan. *Your challenge: Check out the Internet. Start with the* Creating Keepsakes *website at CreatingKeepsakes.com or visit my blog at ElizabethKartchner.blogspot.com!*

1 When do you find inspiration?
- **A** All the time—almost everything around me provokes an idea.
- **B** When I'm in a creative mood.
- **C** When I'm consciously out looking for ideas.

2 Where do you look for inspiration?
- **A** Scrapbooking magazines and idea books.
- **B** Online galleries, websites and blogs.
- **C** Everywhere—home-decor and fashion magazines, catalogs, billboards—you name it!

3 What do you do with ideas that inspire you?
- **A** I keep an inspiration folder, notebook or bulletin board.
- **B** I mark layouts I like in magazines and idea books.
- **C** I just try to keep them in mind for my next project.

4 Which are you most apt to do?
- **A** Scraplift a layout I like almost directly.
- **B** Take an idea from a layout and tweak it to fit my style or purpose.
- **C** Come up with my own ideas and techniques.

5 Which best describes your creative process?
- **A** I flip through my files or magazines to see what strikes me.
- **B** I look through my photos, choose a topic and often look for a sketch as a design template.
- **C** My mind is teeming with cool ideas, so when it's time to create, I get right to it!

ANSWERS: 1. A-3, B-2, C-1; 2. A-1, B-2, C-3; 3. A-3, B-1, C-2; 4. A-1, B-2, C-3; 5. A-2, B-1, C-3.

LIZZY'S LAST WORD:

Get inspired

We all have moments when we aren't feeling it. Like you, I sometimes need to recharge my creative batteries. Here's what I do to intentionally seek and consciously recognize inspiration:

- **HEAD ONLINE.** I know I can count on finding something cool on home-decor and fashion sites. These are some of my favorite destinations:

  Design Sponge (DesignSpongeonline.com)— cool color combinations, luscious fabric patterns and juicy pictures that make me happy.

  Anthropologie (Anthropologie.com)—always on-trend fashions with a funky, homespun vibe.

  Polyvore (Polyvore.com)—sensory-rich playground for imaginative fashionistas and closet interior designers like me.

- **PICK UP A MAGAZINE.** There's something about settling in with a glossy magazine that really lights my fire. Specifically, I'm a big fan of these publications:

  Creating Keepsakes—the number-one source for scrapbooking goodness.

  Cookie—a mom's dreamland full of color and energy.

  Martha Stewart Living—iconic for a reason. Martha's magazine is always exquisite.

- **KEEP A RECORD OF THINGS THAT INSPIRE YOU.** I'm constantly printing up something I've found online or ripping pages out of magazines.

- **GO WITH THE FLOW.** If I'm not feeling inspired, I've learned not to force it. Remember, once you give in to negativity, it sucks the creativity out of you. Try sitting down and designing a card or a very simple layout design to get the creative juices flowing.

- **CULTIVATE CREATIVITY.** Try something new. Take a class to learn some new skills. You may find something new that you love.

take a number

You probably don't think too much about numbers in relation to scrapbooking, unless you're counting your supplies or measuring something for your layout. But our mathematical friends can come in handy in countless (get it?) ways. In this chapter, we'll harness the power of numbers!

6 Use a specific time as your layout's title.

If you're like me, your life is dictated by schedules. At our house, we have a very definite routine and rhythm we follow, and certain things happen at certain times every day. For your next layout, why not freeze a moment in time and dedicate a page to that particular time of day?

Kelly's layout cracks me up! The photo was taken with a fisheye lens, which gives the whole page an eccentric vibe. Her reference to the time makes an ironic statement about the "glamorous" life of these two city-dwellers. Also, did you spot her subtle cardstock treatment? She simply layered die-cut shapes atop background paper of the same color. Such a fresh look!

Ten O'Clock by Kelly Purkey.
Supplies Cardstock: American Crafts; Patterned paper: American Crafts (zebra) and October Afternoon (red); Die-cut machine: Making Memories; Rub-ons: Doodlebug Design; Brads: American Crafts; Tag: Creative Café, Creative Imaginations; Corner rounder: Fiskars Americas; Font: American Typewriter; Other: Thread.

I love candid photos. When people aren't posing or clowning for the camera, reality happens. This picture perfectly depicts the daily reunion between my daughter, Avery, and my husband, Collin. It's a precious recurring moment for our family, and now we have a record of it. For a fun design idea, try journaling in a circle and adding your title in the center.

5:24 *by Elizabeth Kartchner.* **Supplies** *Patterned paper:* BasicGrey and KI Memories; *Number stickers and brads:* American Crafts; *Letter stickers:* Glitz Designs; *House sticker:* KI Memories; *Font:* You Are Loved; *Adhesive:* Glue Dots International and Scrapbook Adhesives by 3L; *Other:* Heart accent.

Bold Eggs *by Cindy Tobey.* **Supplies** *Cardstock:* Bazzill Basics Paper; *Patterned paper:* Fancy Pants Designs; *Letters:* American Crafts ("Eggs") and Making Memories ("Bold"); *Flag banner:* Creative Imaginations; *Journaling spot:* Heidi Swapp for Advantus; *Ribbon:* Cosmo Cricket (green stripe), Making Memories (orange and blue stripe), Mrs. Grossman's (blue dot and yellow dot), Pebbles Inc. (red dot) and Stampin' Up! (solid green); *Chipboard stars:* American Crafts (light green and light blue), Die Cuts With a View (green and blue glitter), Fancy Pants Designs (orange) and Scrapworks (yellow); *Brads:* Bo-Bunny Press (large red dot) and Queen & Co. (all others); *Buttons:* Autumn Leaves; *Paint:* Making Memories; *Glitter:* Doodlebug Design; *Pen:* Sakura; *Font:* Century Gothic; *Other:* Thread and crayon.

7 Celebrate the number seven.

Lots of people consider seven to be a lucky number. I don't know about that, but I do believe that odd numbers work well in design. For this challenge, then, why not try using seven of something on a page? Or go "all in" and use seven of everything on your layout. Have fun!

Whoa! This design puts me in seventh heaven! Can you spot all the items in doses of seven on Cindy's page? List them here:

1 _____

2 _____

3 _____

4 _____

5 _____

6 _____

ANSWERS: 7 photos, 7 buttons, 7 ribbons, 7 brads, 7 flags in the banner sticker and 7 colors (including black and white)

Try this:

CREATE A PAINT-RESIST BACKGROUND

Give a colorful, painted area a bit of texture and interest with this quick and easy technique. You can even customize your pattern to suit the subject of your layout.

1 Use a clear or white crayon to draw designs in each column.

2 Paint over the design with watered-down acrylic paint. When paint is dry, use a dry paper towel to rub over the painted area to bring out the crayon design.

3 Embellish with accents in coordinating hues of the paint color.

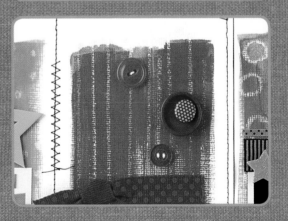

WINK WINK

"I accidently ate all the mint oreos that were in the cupboard. Ooops."

"My house is always spotless and ready for my mother-in-law to come over."

"I don't have a hidden candy stash that I eat when Avery is taking a nap!"

"I won't buy anymore scrapbook supplies until I use the stash I have."

"I will start my healthy eating habits tomorrow."

"Collin, aren't these shoes cute? They were on sale."

"I promise this is the last scrapbook page I'm doing tonight."

When you use a number as your inspiration, you can go all out, as in Cindy's design, or use subtle amounts, like I've done here. I doubt that anyone who looked at my layout would immediately detect how I adapted the challenge on this page, but come closer, and I'll share my secret with you. See it? Seven strips of patterned paper with seven journaling statements beneath seven black acrylic accents. By simply starting with a certain number of a few things, you can come up with a super-cute page!

Wink, Wink by Elizabeth Kartchner. **Supplies** Cardstock and letters: American Crafts; Patterned paper: BasicGrey, KI Memories and Sassafras; Flowers: Prima; Butterfly clip: KI Memories; Font: Kelly's Writing; Adhesive: Glue Dots International and Scrapbook Adhesives by 3L; Other: Black acrylic accents, rhinestones, epoxy border stickers, ribbon and thread.

8 Use all 26 letters of the alphabet.

In a way, this challenge could be a design challenge as well! The sky's the limit for how you meet the challenge . . . will you incorporate the letters into your journaling, employ them as embellishments, spell out something in particular? Let's see what you can do!

No one I'd rather be with than you.

Nothing else matters but that we are together!

No time for work & emails-let's go play!

Boy, did I embrace this challenge or what? No subtlety here. Sometimes it's fun to just go for it, which is why I completely focused the layout on the alphabet idea. Want to try something similar? Replace some of the letters with photos of a person whose name starts with that initial.

No. 4 by Elizabeth Kartchner. **Supplies** Patterned paper: Daisy D's Paper Co. (yellow) and Jenni Bowlin Studio (blue dot); Foam hearts and rub-ons: American Crafts; Chipboard letters: BasicGrey; Font: Century Gothic; Other: Paint and thread.

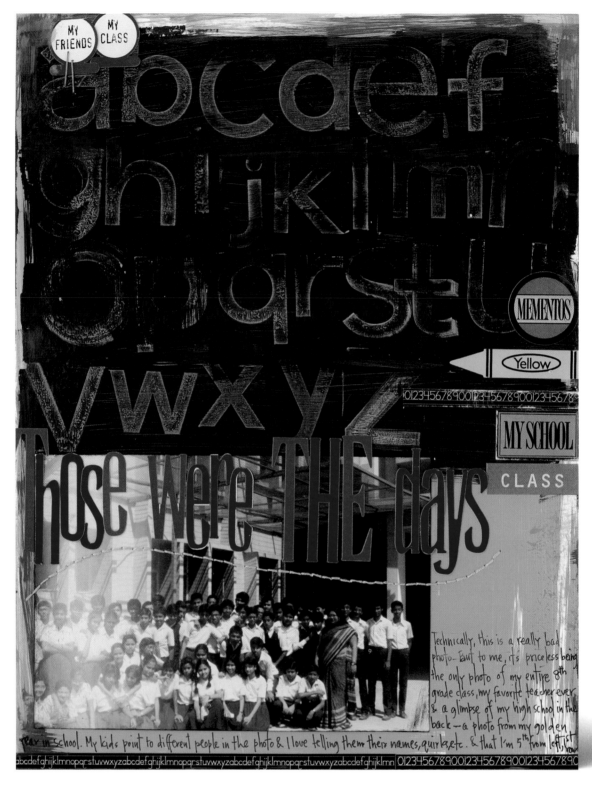

Ah, a school-themed page is perfect for an alphabet challenge. But instead of creating a cute kindergarten page about her son, Mou dipped back into her own past to document a very special time in her life. Don't you just love her cool paint technique? She laid down a thickish layer of paint and then pressed letter stamps into the wet paint and removed them immediately. This exposed the color beneath, creating a muted impression of the letters.

Those Were the Days by Mou Saha.
Supplies *Cardstock:* Frances Meyer; *Stickers:* 7gypsies (school theme) and Rusty Pickle (title); *Paint:* Delta Creative, Making Memories and Matisse Derivan; *Stamps:* Stampin' Up!; *Embroidery floss:* DMC; *Pen:* American Crafts; *Other:* Staples.

9 Create an itemized list.

Are you a list-maker? I love to write down everything, from tasks to favorites to dreams. For this challenge, come up with an interesting numbered list, or incorporate an existing list into your layout design or theme.

The list format is ideally suited for a whimsical layout like mine, which celebrates our family's weakness for cotton candy. I chose to record five things we love about it, since odd numbers tend to work best in design. Without the visual weight of a paragraph, the list feels airy and light, adding to the overall feel of my page.

Yum Yum *by Elizabeth Kartchner.* **Supplies** *Patterned paper:* American Crafts and KI Memories; *Acrylic paper and sticker:* KI Memories; *Letters, photo corners and button:* American Crafts; *Arrows:* Sassafras; *Font:* AL Uncle Charles; *Adhesive:* Glue Dots International and Scrapbook Adhesives by 3L; *Other:* Circle punch.

I am extremely stubborn.

I watch too much TV.

I procrastinate, a lot.

I love to sleep.

I get a headache when I'm hungry.

I believe in love at first sight.
(am married to the 'said' love now)

I have to get my feet covered,
especially when I'm in bed.

I indulge in chocolate
at least once a day.

I am a klutz. Total klutz.

nine facts

Many scrapbookers hesitate to make layouts about themselves, but we really must! Someday our children will want to know what we were like when they were growing up. No children? Don't you want a record of who you were and what was important to you at this point in your life? Plus, it doesn't need to be anything heavy or deep. Do like Sasha did and scrap a page about a few of your quirks or characteristics— embrace the randomness of it all!

Nine Facts by Sasha Farina. **Supplies** *Cardstock:* Bazzill Basics Paper; *Patterned paper:* Making Memories (red flocked dot) and Sassafras (lined and brown); *Flowers:* Prima; *Chipboard accents:* BasicGrey; *Tags:* Creative Imaginations; *Sticker:* Daisy D's Paper Co.; *Stamp:* Label Tulip; *Ink:* VersaMark, Tsukineko; *Glitter spray:* Glimmer Mist, Tattered Angels; *Pearl medium and glitter:* Liquid Pearls and Stickles, Ranger Industries; *Font:* Rough Typewriter; *Other:* Buttons.

Try this:

ENHANCE EMBELLISHMENTS FOR A ONE-OF-A-KIND LOOK

Part of the appeal of Sasha's style is how she dresses up premade accents. Did you notice the little touches that personalize her page?

1 Give a chipboard accent some extra pizzazz with a glimmery top coat.

2 Create a layered focal point with stamping, title letters, buttons and pearly droplets.

3 Add impact to paper flowers with a few strokes of glitter glue.

10 Time's up!
Finish a page in 30 minutes.

Oh, goodness. If you're anything like me, you tend to belabor paper selection and other design and embellishment decisions way too long. So let's light a fire under our chairs and start cranking something out! You may find that when you don't overanalyze the process, you instinctively allow your creativity to take over.

When your aim is to make efficient use of time, you must take advantage of premade products. In this case, a journaling spot and a premade title helped my page come together in a snap. To inject visual interest without a huge time investment, use a shaped background paper.

Silly by Elizabeth Kartchner. **Supplies** *Patterned paper:* Cosmo Cricket and Jenni Bowlin Studio; *Chipboard and felt letters:* KI Memories; *Stickers:* Cosmo Cricket; *Pen:* American Crafts; *Adhesive:* Glue Dots International and Scrapbook Adhesives by 3L.

Not only do you adore spending time together, but you are so very much alike. You both share the same positive attitude, and love for life. You can always be found looking on the bright side of things, with a smile on your face & a skip in your step. Whenever you're together, it's happiness x's 2.

Sheri's secret to a quick layout was to create a smaller page within a larger one. She trimmed her scalloped cardstock to 10" x 10" and designed the layout using the smaller canvas. After adhering her patterned papers and photos, she attached the smaller page to a 12" x 12" background. With a final flourish of ribbon and a few long journaling strips, she was done!

So Happy Together by Sheri Reguly. **Supplies** *Cardstock:* Bazzill Basics Paper; *Patterned paper:* Bo-Bunny Press and KI Memories; *Ribbon:* KI Memories; *Sticker:* Doodlebug Design; *Chipboard accents:* Chatterbox; *Brads:* American Crafts; *Fonts:* Print Clearly (title) and Times New Roman.

11 Time's up!
Finish a page in 45 minutes.

Phew! Let's continue this time limit idea, but this time, I'll give you a few extra minutes. You'll still need to streamline your process, but you have time for some extra touches. Let's see what you can do.

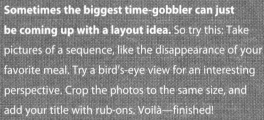

Sometimes the biggest time-gobbler can just be coming up with a layout idea. So try this: Take pictures of a sequence, like the disappearance of your favorite meal. Try a bird's-eye view for an interesting perspective. Crop the photos to the same size, and add your title with rub-ons. Voilà—finished!

Going, Going, Gone by Elizabeth Kartchner. **Supplies** *Patterned paper:* Creative Imaginations and October Afternoon; *Letters, rub-ons, brads and pen:* American Crafts; *Border punch:* Fiskars Americas; *Stamp:* Making Memories; *Ink:* StazOn, Tsukineko; *Adhesive:* Glue Dots International and Scrapbook Adhesives by 3L; *Other:* Label.

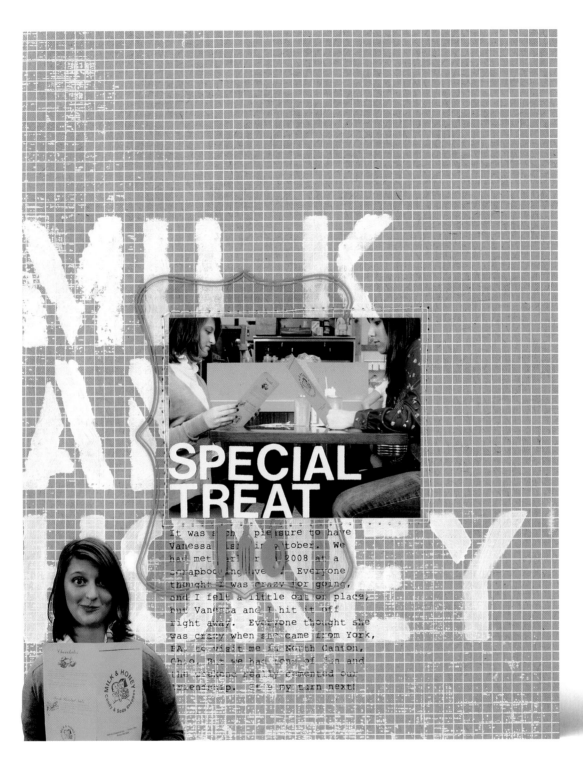

SPECIAL TREAT

It was such a pleasure to have Vanessa visit in October. We had met earlier in 2008 at a scrapbooking event. Everyone thought I was crazy for going, and I felt a little out of place, but Vanessa and I hit it off right away. Everyone thought she was crazy when she came from York, PA, to visit me in North Canton, Ohio. But we had tons of fun and the weekend really cemented our friendship. It's my turn next!

You may be tempted to avoid wet mediums when your timetable is tight, but Amanda proves that it can be done! She used a heavy white acrylic paint and a stencil brush to put the name of the restaurant, Milk and Honey, onto the background. Acrylic paint dries quickly, so she was able to layer her photos, journaling and embellishments right over it. Double-duty—the stenciled title conveys information and adds a cool graphic look!

Special Treat by Amanda Johnson.
Supplies *Patterned paper and transparency:* Hambly Screen Prints; *Font:* Rough Typewriter; *Other:* Stencils, paint and thread.

12 Time's up!
Finish a page in 60 minutes.

OK, just one more. With a full hour, you should be able to whip out something really special. Work steadily and be aware of the clock, but you do have a bit of a cushion, so let your imagination take flight.

I'm a sucker for a thumb sucker! The best is when she sucks on her thumb and lays her head on my chest at the same time! It's precious!!

She melts my heart everytime she sticks that little thumb in her mouth. I am literally putty in her hands! Especially when she pulls her blankie to her cheek.

Would it shock you to know that I rarely actually finish a page in less than an hour? I tend to move things around on the paper and scrutinize everything about my layout—it's exhausting! Having the time limit really forced me to work efficiently. By repeating a scalloped punch shape in various colors and patterns, I achieved a quick design that allowed me time to add sparkle to some of my embellishments.

Melts My Heart by Elizabeth Kartchner. **Supplies** *Patterned paper:* BasicGrey, Crate Paper and KI Memories; *Letters:* Making Memories; *Chipboard:* KI Memories; *Felt:* Fancy Pants Designs; *Glitter:* Stickles, Ranger Industries; *Font:* Century Gothic; *Adhesive:* Glue Dots International and Scrapbook Adhesives by 3L; *Other:* Scallop-edged circle punch and thread.

I absolutely "love, cherish and adore" how Keisha used a line to serve as a design base, journaling spot and accent effect all at the same time. The trimmed paper strips, flowers and tags create a girly, pretty border for her lovely layout, while the vellum layer keeps the mood soft as it accentuates her focal-point photograph. It's not an overly complicated page, but it's ever so striking, isn't it?

Love Cherish Adore by Keisha Campbell. **Supplies** *Cardstock:* Creative Imaginations (brown floral) and Making Memories (journal sheets); *Ribbon, punch, tags, paper flags and flowers:* Martha Stewart Crafts; *Stamps, buttons and brads:* Making Memories; *Other:* Vellum.

Quiz:
We've got your number!

For this quiz, you're going to need to pull out your albums. Let's see what you've really been working on, and what the numbers say about you.

Once you've completed the quiz, you can use it as a tool for self-reflection. Do you like your totals? Do you sense any gaps in the topics you're scrapping? Would you like to stretch yourself more by attempting layouts in a format you haven't really tried?

On the lines below, jot down any reactions you may have to the numbers you've come up with. Then, write down any goals you may want to pursue in light of your totals. No pressure, though—feel free to just mosey on along to the next page and be done with it!

_____

_____

_____

_____

_____

_____

1 How many of your albums fall into the following categories?

___ Themed (wedding, vacation, friends, etc.)

___ Random collections of layouts (including chronological)

2 How many total layouts have you completed over the years?

___ 0–20   ___ 100–200

___ 20–50   ___ More than 200

___ 50–100

3 What are the topics of your layouts? How many layouts fall into each of the following categories? *Note: Don't put the same layout into more than one category. Decide which category is the best fit.*

___ My children   ___ Special occasions
                               (birthdays, weddings,
___ My husband or   holidays, etc.)
    immediate family
                           ___ Nature or seasons
___ Me
                           ___ Daily life
___ Friends
                           ___ Other
___ Extended family

___ Vacations

4 How many pictures do you use on each layout? Indicate your totals below.

___ 1   ___ 4–7

___ 2–3   ___ 8 or more

5 How many layouts do you have in each of these formats?

___ 12" x 12"   ___ 8½" x 11"
    double-page spreads   single-page spreads

___ 12" x 12"   ___ Other
    single-page spreads

___ 8½" x 11"
    double-page spreads

LIZZY'S LAST WORD:

By the numbers

- Number of 12" x 12" albums I've filled: 22

- Number of hours I spend on average designing a layout: 3

- Number of gummy bears I consume while I work on a layout: 34

- Number of times Avery has sabotaged a layout: **Only once,** thank goodness

- How often I purge supplies and bring my sister a box of goodies: **Every six months**

- Number of different paint colors I tried for my scrap room before finding the perfect sun-washed blue: 6

- Latest time I've stayed up scrapbooking? **1:30 a.m.** (A rare occasion—I'm not a night owl.)

- How often I ask Collin if he likes my finished scrapbook page: **Every time**

- How often Collin says he likes my finished scrapbook page: **Every time**

- Number of times I pause to check on Quincey while I'm creating: 3

- Number of sets of alphabets I have in my current stash: 174

- How long my desk stays clean after I finish a project: **20 minutes**

- How often I still pinch myself that I'm blessed to share my ideas with you: **Every day**

design & color

We're all creatures of habit. It's perfectly fine to rely on go-to design schemes or color combinations. But shaking things up is healthy and necessary for growth. Get ready to stretch yourself a little in this chapter!

13 Combine black and white and color.

Black and white is a graphic and classic color scheme. For this challenge, start with black and white and contrast it with a pop of glorious color.

Choosing my accent color for this page was a no-brainer, since Avery was wearing pink in the photo. The beauty of this challenge is that most photographs naturally provide light and dark areas, so nabbing this color scheme is easy and a sure-fire winner, no matter what additional color you add to the palette.

Angel in Disguise by Elizabeth Kartchner. **Supplies** *Patterned paper:* Heidi Swapp for Advantus and KI Memories; *Letters:* October Afternoon; *Transparency:* Hambly Screen Prints; *Rhinestones and rub-ons:* Glitz Design; *Felt:* Fancy Pants Designs; *Acrylic wing:* Heidi Swapp for Advantus; *Buttons:* Chatterbox; *Font:* 2Peas Tubby; *Adhesive:* Glue Dots International and Scrapbook Adhesives by 3L; *Other:* Pen and thread.

Don't be afraid to interpret the challenges your own way! Kelly went in a totally different direction by mixing color with black-and-white photographs. Look at that stunning, large photo—setting it against the bright, fun colors of the rest of the layout really makes it stand out.

Winter Wonderland by Kelly Purkey. **Supplies** *Cardstock, buttons, decorative scissors, pen and adhesive:* American Crafts; *Patterned paper:* American Crafts (stripe), Doodlebug Design (pink) and Heidi Grace Designs (snowflakes); *Stickers:* Heidi Grace Designs; *Die-cutting machine:* Making Memories; *Rhinestones:* Hero Arts; *Other:* Thread.

Extra Long *by Cindy Tobey.* **Supplies** *Patterned paper:* BasicGrey (cream, brown dot), Luxe Designs (blue lined, tan print) and Scenic Route (brown leaves); *Sticker:* Love, Elsie for KI Memories; *Chipboard:* BasicGrey (letters and star), me & my BIG ideas (large circle) and Scenic Route (circle frames); *Ribbon:* SEI; *Buttons:* Autumn Leaves; *Ink:* Clearsnap; *Paint:* Making Memories; *Circle cutter:* Creative Memories; *Circle punches:* EK Success; *Font:* Arial Narrow; *Other:* Thread and yarn.

14 Play around with circles.

There's just something fun about the curve of a circle. Because photographs are linear, we're accustomed to designing in straight lines. So I challenge you to make an all-circular layout. Yep, sometimes going around in circles can be a good thing!

Cindy really rounded up her creativity for this one! Though her layout is square, she added a large patterned-paper circle to it. Notice how she used lots of circular embellishments and cut her photos into circles. She even cut a round "e" out of her large photo and chose a rounded font for her title stickers to carry through the circular theme.

I totally love how all the circles on my layout complement the shape of the berries as well as the buttons on Avery's jacket. Even the non-circular accents, like the clouds and mushrooms and rainbows, are rounded. Dot paper and a curved title, too—yes, I was into this challenge! Oh, and did you notice how I journaled in the negative space on one of my photos?

Berry Pickin' *by Elizabeth Kartchner.* **Supplies** *Cardstock:* Bazzill Basics Paper; *Patterned paper:* KI Memories, October Afternoon and Sassafras; *Letters:* American Crafts; *Strawberries:* Martha Stewart Crafts; *Font:* Peaches; *Adhesive:* Glue Dots International and Scrapbook Adhesives by 3L.

15 Stick to a single color.

Limiting your design choices can sometimes be very liberating. When you pare down the world of possibilities, you may find that you eliminate a lot of the decision-making that goes into page creation. So, for this challenge, I want you to go for a monochromatic color scheme. The color choice is up to you!

A monochromatic page can help retain the focus when you have lots of lively photographs. Even a powerful and energetic hue like red competes less with the photos for attention than if it were paired with other colors.

Traditions by Elizabeth Kartchner. **Supplies** *Cardstock:* Bazzill Basics Paper; *Patterned paper:* American Crafts and Scenic Route; *Letters:* American Crafts; *Stickers:* Scenic Route; *Flowers:* Prima; *Ribbon, epoxy tag and brads:* Making Memories; *Tags and tickets:* Shabby Chic Crafts; *Font:* Century Gothic; *Adhesive:* Glue Dots International and Scrapbook Adhesives by 3L.

It's not tough to figure out how Keisha went about choosing the color for her monochromatic layout. By tying the color scheme to her daughter's hair decorations, the focus of the page lands squarely on Mikiela's beautiful face!

Delightful Everyday *by Keisha Campbell.* **Supplies** *Patterned paper:* BasicGrey (teal background) and Making Memories (dot, floral); *Flowers, letter stickers and buttons:* Making Memories; *Stamps:* Hero Arts; *Punches:* Marvy Uchida (scallop circle) and Stampin' Up! (scallop border); *Other:* Font, ink and straight pins.

16 Use the shape of your journaling as a design element.

It's easy to think of journaling as merely a way to convey information on a layout, but you can also put it to work as an added visual element on your page. For this challenge, arrange your words in a shape that reinforces the theme of your design!

My little Avery is such a chatterbox! She cracks me up, and half the time I can't even follow her train of thought. I wanted to remember her toddler talkativity, so I formatted the journaling in swirls of squished type to imitate her non-stop, sometimes hard-to-decipher monologues.

Big Things to Say by Elizabeth Kartchner. **Supplies** *Cardstock:* Bazzill Basics Paper; *Patterned paper:* Heidi Swapp for Advantus, KI Memories and Sassafras; *Letters:* American Crafts and Making Memories; *Rub-on:* Jenni Bowlin Studio; *Plastic stickers:* KI Memories; *Digital frame:* Skinny Label + Paper Freebie by Jennifer Pebbles; *Digital lace:* Digital Scrapbooking Day Freebie by Danielle Thompson; *Adhesive:* Glue Dots International and Scrapbook Adhesives by 3L; *Other:* Font.

Try this:

CREATE JOURNALING SWIRLS

If you have Photoshop, you can replicate my technique easily. If you don't have this software, try sketching lines with a pencil and handwriting your journaling along the path.

1 First, click on the Pen tool and click on the Paths button in the Options bar at the top of the screen (the icon looks like a pen with a square around it).

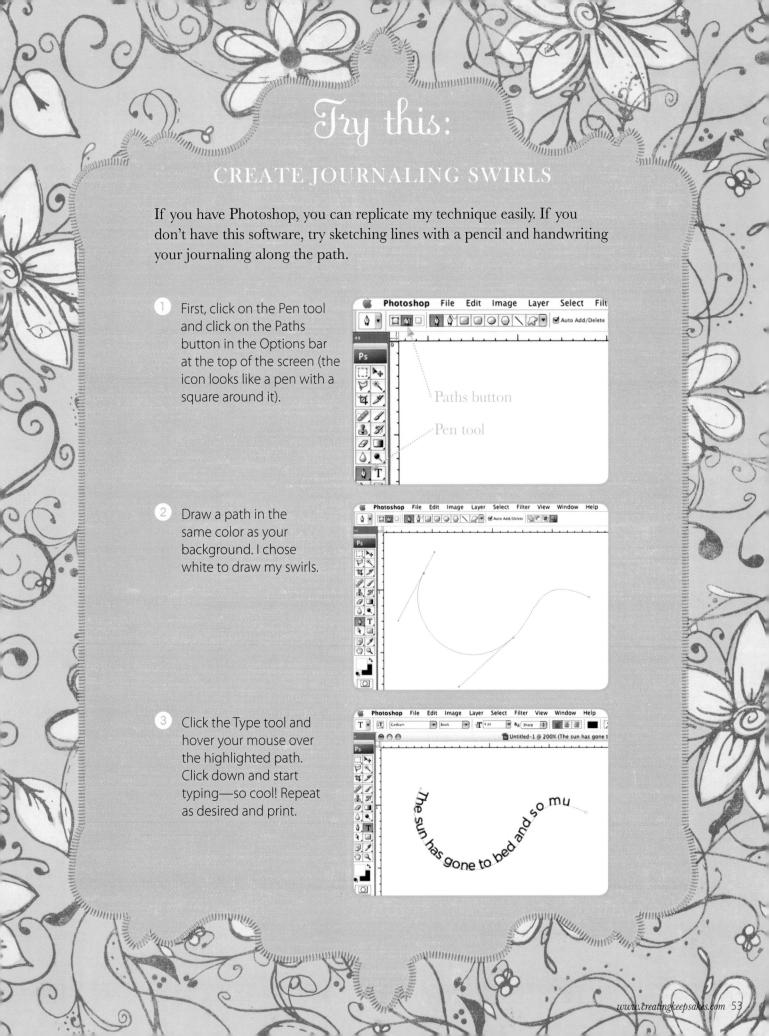

Paths button

Pen tool

2 Draw a path in the same color as your background. I chose white to draw my swirls.

3 Click the Type tool and hover your mouse over the highlighted path. Click down and start typing—so cool! Repeat as desired and print.

The sun has gone to bed and so mu

JUMP

BODY IN MOTION

KNOWS NO BOUNDS

ENTHUSIASTIC

THE REAL DEAL

RIGHT STUFF

UNFORGETTABLE

Om, Gatlinburg, TN, 10/27/06

Ever since Nini read Vera Rosenberry's Whiz Splash, a book about nature's beauty through the seasons & how kids can enjoy each, she's been mentioning that Florida is no fun as there are no colorful crunchy leaves to jump into in Fall or smooth silvery ice to whiz through in Winter. When we went on our Fall road trip to the Smoky Mountains this October, the kids kept looking for a yard with a big, inviting pile of raked leaves but saw none. Finally, at the Gatlinburg Visitor Center, Om spotted small piles of fallen leaves scattered around the parking lot. On that 30°F Fall morning, he stepped out & jumped on them to his heart's content & chased them as the wind blew them away. Joy glowed on his flushed little face.

Mou wanted to include a page element related to autumn, so she wrote her journaling on a leaf die cut. Design-wise, her journaling spot visually extends the fallen leaves in the photos onto her layout. The tissues, crepe papers, stitching and glitter spray all combine to mirror the colors and textures we associate with fall.

Jump *by Mou Saha.* **Supplies** *Cardstock:* Frances Meyer; *Patterned paper and tags:* Rusty Pickle; *Stickers:* 7gypsies (cardstock) and Rusty Pickle (title); *Leaf die cuts:* Sizzix, Provo Craft; *Embroidery floss:* DMC; *Pen:* American Crafts; *Other:* Staples and crepe paper.

17 Tilt your design on an angle.

Ah, I know you. Always sticking to the straight and narrow. I challenge you to bend a little! Allow your design to slant—you just may love what happens!

I just love the energy of this page, and I really think the angled design is part of its appeal. I made sure to ground my design with the coordinating sets of layered embellishments. Don't be afraid to layer paper onto buttons, stickers or chipboard, or to layer a title on top of a photo.

Sparkle *by Elizabeth Kartchner.* **Supplies** *Patterned paper:* Daisy D's Paper Co., Doodlebug Design, KI Memories and Making Memories; *Letters:* Making Memories; *Stickers:* American Crafts; *Journaling tag:* My Mind's Eye; *Buttons:* Autumn Leaves (clear) and Sassafras (pink); *Font:* Cooper Std Black; *Adhesive:* Glue Dots International and Scrapbook Adhesives by 3L; *Other:* Heart button, thread and ribbon.

It was a treacherous climb, but you were up for the challenge!

DESTINATION:
You started out slow, made it up the steep incline a bit, and then your footing slipped and you slid down, completely losing the altitude you had gained. This happened again and again, until finally, you did it! You made it to the summit of Mt. Slide! You whooped it up and then took in the splendor that the view had to offer from the summit... and then, you slid all the way back down...so you could climb and defeat Mt. Slide yet again!

SCENIC OVERLOOK

the SUMMIT

10.22.08

Slanting the elements on this layout wasn't a random design choice for Cindy, since it related well to the theme of her son scrambling up a steep slide. Since her photos were taken on an angle, tilting them actually makes her son Elijah appear upright. Notice that on both of our layouts, we didn't just angle things willy-nilly—we took the entire design and shifted it.

The Summit by Cindy Tobey. **Supplies** *Cardstock:* WorldWin; *Patterned paper:* Making Memories; *Tags:* Luxe Designs (circle) and Making Memories (red); *Chipboard:* American Crafts (letters); Love, Elsie for KI Memories (button); *Metal sign:* K&Company; *Rub-ons:* Colorbök (compass) and Love, Elsie for KI Memories (red doodle); *Ribbon:* Pebbles Inc.; *Paint:* Making Memories; *Button:* Fancy Pants Designs; *Brad:* Queen & Co.; *Ink:* Clearsnap; *Pen:* Sakura; *Font:* Insonorm; *Other:* Staples and thread.

18 Go fishing for complements.

Do you know your color theory? On the color wheel, every color has its very own complementary color—the hue directly opposite it on the wheel. Pairing complementary colors is a no-fail choice for injecting energy and contrast into your designs. Try a complementary color scheme today!

Red and green don't just work together at Christmastime—they complement one another year round. For this page about our daily routine, I converted a couple of my photos to black and white to avoid competing with my star colors. Hidden journaling details our typical schedule.

Routine by Elizabeth Kartchner. **Supplies** *Patterned paper:* KI Memories (calendar), Prima (green) and Sassafras (rainbow); *Felt flower, pen, vinyl sign and car:* American Crafts; *Clip:* Making Memories.

so very proud

You did so well in the year end exam!

Congrats Girl!

Just because you're going complementary doesn't mean you're stuck with a two-color layout. Sasha tossed in bits of red and green to spice up her blue-and-orange page. To expand her design choices, she layered a blue birdcage transparency atop orange cardstock for a vibrant effect.

So Very Proud by Sasha Farina. **Supplies** *Cardstock:* Bazzill Basics Paper; *Patterned paper:* Jenni Bowlin Studio (blue bracket), Making Memories (red flock) and Scenic Route (gray grid); *Transparency:* Hambly Screen Prints; *Flowers and felt accent:* Prima; *Rhinestones:* Heidi Swapp for Advantus (white) and Prima (orange); *Chipboard accents:* Heidi Grace Designs; *Stamps:* Label Tulip (wood grain) and Stampin' Up! ("happy thoughts"); *Brads:* Making Memories; *Letter stickers:* American Crafts; *Epoxy accents:* Ranger Industries; *Font:* Traveling Typewriter.

19 Incorporate 10 or more photos on a layout.

Can you create a page with lots of pictures that doesn't look cluttered? Using multiple photos in a clean design is definitely a challenge, but I know you can do it! (Note: For more number-oriented challenges, turn to Chapter 2.)

Don't be afraid to crop photos and mix picture sizes on your layout. When all the photographs are the same size, your eye might have a hard time knowing where to look. On this layout, I also tried to arrange my pictures in the timeline at the bottom of my page to show the sequence of the events I documented.

Swim, Bike, Run *by Elizabeth Kartchner.* **Supplies** *Cardstock:* Bazzill Basics Paper; *Lace cardstock:* KI Memories; *Patterned paper and letters:* American Crafts; *Rub-ons:* Glitz Designs; *Font:* You Are Loved; *Other:* Circle punch.

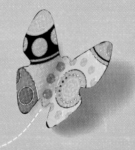

Leaves *by Cindy Tobey.* **Supplies** *Cardstock:* Bazzill Basics Paper; *Patterned paper:* Bo-Bunny Press (yellow dot), Cosmo Cricket (clouds, leaves, plaid, red and wood grain), Crate Paper (scallop grid) and My Mind's Eye (yellow large dot); *Chipboard:* American Crafts (letters), Making Memories ("all boy"), Maya Road (arrow) and SEI (circle with leaf); *Rub-ons:* Colorbök ("adventure"), Cosmo Cricket (label) and Hambly Screen Prints (leaves); *Ribbon:* Rusty Pickle; *Ink:* Clearsnap; *Pen:* Sakura; *Font:* Century Schoolbook; *Other:* Cork and thread.

When working with a double-page spread, Cindy likes to lay out her photos on a 17" x 11" canvas in Photoshop Elements. She finds it especially helpful for resizing pictures and designing with a lot of photographs. How cool is it that even with 10 photos on the page (not to mention journaling and a fun tree accent), she had plenty of room for resting space? By the way, that tree? Cindy applied a rub-on to cork for the trunk, and applied rub-ons to patterned paper for the leaves. How stinkin' awesome is that?

Try this:

ACHIEVE EFFECTIVE MULTIPHOTO DESIGN

Check out these tips for working with numerous photos. Good design makes all the difference!

1. Include a mix of full-length and detail shots.

2. Use a circle punch to add variety to your design. Intersperse photos and embellishments.

3. Choose a focal-point photo and emphasize it by making it larger than the other photos on the page.

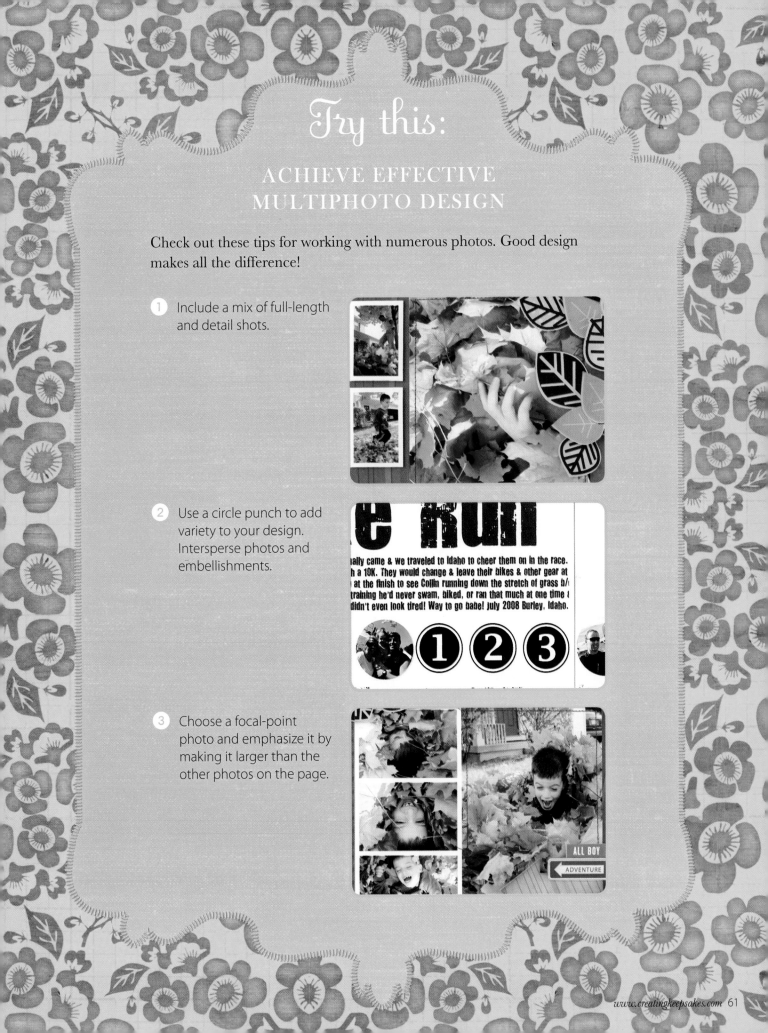

e Run

ally came & we traveled to Idaho to cheer them on in the race. h a 10K. They would change & leave their bikes & other gear at at the finish to see Collin running down the stretch of grass b/c training he'd never swam, biked, or ran that much at one time a didn't even look tired! Way to go babe! July 2008 Burley, Idaho.

ALL BOY
ADVENTURE

20 Use a grid as the basis for a page design.

Architects use grids to sketch out their designs, so why not build your page on a grid? You'll find everything lining up nicely with a grid as your foundation, and coming up with the design for your layout won't seem so overwhelming.

I've always liked layouts that allow me to get a lot of different events scrapped at once. That's one of the things I really adore about Beth's layout. To document an entire month on one page, she determined that the calendar-grid format would provide nice lines for her photo placement. She positioned pictures atop the dates when the events occurred. Try replicating this layout for a year's worth of months and putting them in an album.

October 2008 by Beth Opel. **Supplies** Cardstock: Bazzill Basics Paper; Patterned paper: Bo-Bunny Press (blue dot) and Scenic Route (floral); Epoxy sticker: KI Memories; Flower: Daisy D's Paper Co.; Brads: Little Yellow Bicycle (fabric) and Making Memories (all others); Pinking shears: Fiskars Americas; Fiber: Maya Road; Fonts: French Script (title) and Rockwell (journaling); Other: Chipboard bookplate.

look who's 2!

can't believe my little girl is 2! We had a blast celebrating your special day! Everyone came over to our house and the theme was pink piggies, since that is your current obsession. I don't know why but you love pigs a lot. You also love Aerial from the Disney movie, The Little Mermaid. There was a lot of people here to celebrate. Aunt Em, Uncle Russ, Auntie Ashley, Uncle Chris, Uncle Josh, Uncle KC, J, Yaya, Auntie Camille, Uncle Matt, ofcourse your cousin Matty, Gigi, Aunt Bebe and Uncle Casey. You were silly when you opened up your presents and yelled 'Edie' at your multiple Aerial presents. I want you to know how much all your family loves you and everyone was so happy to be here to celebrate. You had a heart shaped cake with flowers on it. You loved eating the frosting and cake-just like your momma! You had a blast playing with your new kitchen & Dora bike. may 2008.

For my version of the grid design, I imagined lines on my page and arranged punched scalloped circles in rows and columns. The roundness of the shapes is a nice contrast to the linear design. By layering punched shapes, I added dimension and fun with colorful patterned papers and playful embellishments to fit the birthday theme.

Look Who's 2 by Elizabeth Kartchner. **Supplies** Cardstock: Bazzill Basics Paper; Patterned paper: Jenni Bowlin Studio, Prima and Sassafras; Letters: American Crafts and SEI; Stickers: American Crafts; Chipboard: Sassafras; Layered button flower: Evalicious, Etsy. com; Font: Sailboat; Adhesive: Glue Dots International and Scrapbook Adhesives by 3L; Other: Scalloped circle punches and pen.

Quiz:
What's your design & color IQ?

Choose the letter of the best answer and check your answers to find out how savvy you are. No worries if you're still learning—that's what this book is all about!

1. C. If you only had red, yellow and blue paint, you could mix them in various proportions to produce any other color. The secondary colors are created by combining equal parts of two primary colors.

2. B. If everything on a page is the same size, or if something overwhelms and takes attention away from the photos, the layout suffers from visual hierarchy problems. Always try to consider what is most important on a page and make sure it receives the attention and focus it deserves.

3. C. When embellishments are simply attached to a layout in an open spot, they appear to "float." Simply move them to the edge of a page element like a photo, and they'll become grounded and improve the flow of the entire layout.

4. A. While complementary colors are across the color wheel from one another (see p. 57), analogous pairs are next to each other.

5. B. You may know white space as "negative space." Every layout needs a place for the eyes to rest. Allow some white space on your designs for the most pleasing effect.

1 What are the primary and secondary colors?

A Primary: red, green and blue; Secondary: yellow, orange and purple

B Primary: red, blue and yellow; Secondary: black, white and gray

C Primary: red, yellow and blue; Secondary: green, purple and orange

D Primary: chartreuse, magenta and ecru; Secondary: orchid, mauve and tangerine

2 What is a visual hierarchy?

A A fancy design term that basically means the same as "focal point"

B A way of arranging elements on a page in an easily understood order of importance

C A description for a title that is difficult to read against a busy background

D A kingdom where those who wear spectacles hold all the power

3 What does it mean to "ground" embellishments?

A To place them at or near the bottom of a page

B To use an even number of them to retain symmetry

C To overlap them on the edge of photos or other page elements

D To pulverize them in a food processor

4 Which of the following pairs are analogous colors?

A Orange and red

B Green and purple

C Blue and yellow

D Vanna White and Clint Black

5 What is white space?

A The space between words in a journaling block

B An open area on a page with no print or photos

C A calming effect achieved by using white background paper

D The Milky Way, of course!

LIZZY'S
LAST WORD:
Color & design tips

It's always great to try new things and stretch yourself. But when you hit on something that's tried and true—something that works every time—make it a regular part of your process! Over the years I've collected a few go-to design strategies that I use on most of my pages.

- **GALLON/QUART/PINT COLOR BALANCING.** Once you've chosen a color scheme, think about the proportions of each shade that you'll use on your layout. There should be one color that is dominant (gallon), with a smaller amount of another (quart) and just a touch of a third (pint). If you ever look at your page and feel like all the colors are meshed together, try adding a pop of a bright, contrasting color.

- **VISUAL TRIANGLE.** This is such a good one! No more random pages. Lay out your design so that you provide a road map for how to view it. Lead the eye around your page on a strategic path by having three elements of the same color, or three sections of text, or three spots with accent clusters that draw the viewer to each of the important places on your page one at a time.

- **MIX AND MATCH.** There was a time when I struggled with choosing patterned paper. I wanted my pages to be vibrant, but I either tended to select just one pattern, which seemed flat to me, or I'd combine patterns, which felt a bit chaotic. I finally learned that

the key for my style was to mix large patterns with smaller patterns. Now my pages have a controlled sense of fun and a little added visual interest that I really like.

- **ODDBALL.** Remember our visual triangle? Three is a magic number for a reason. The eye responds better to odd-numbered groupings. You may see this in home decor, floral arrangement and photography, and it's just as true for embellishments. I don't know how this works. Maybe with even numbers, we run the risk of splitting a page into halves? Whatever the explanation, I've learned to love being an oddball!

use your stash

I'm a firm believer in making do with what I have. I don't want to rush off to the scrapbook store when I'm in the middle of creating a layout. With a little ingenuity, I can come up with a creative solution using the supplies I already have on hand. You can, too—and these challenges will help get you started!

21 Design your own paper-pieced accent.

Your layouts should reflect your distinctive personality. For this challenge, express yourself with an original accent. Put your supplies to work and make a one-of-a-kind paper embellishment that's worthy of your unique style!

Sometimes I wish time could stand still! That I could hold onto a fleeting moment just a bit longer. I'm always amazed at how fast time goes by & how you grow right before my eyes. Since I can't stop time from passing-I'll just cherish each day!!

One super-easy way to create an original page accent is to cut a favorite section out of patterned paper. To create my cute floral accent, I used a craft knife, but you can accomplish the same look with precise scissors. It just depends on what you're more comfortable with! Give the accent a little extra oomph with the addition of layered stamped images and rub-ons.

Cherish by Elizabeth Kartchner. **Supplies** *Patterned paper:* Crate Paper; *Letters:* Rusty Pickle; *Rub-ons:* Jenni Bowlin Studio; *Flowers:* Making Memories; *Buttons:* KI Memories; *Stamps:* Autumn Leaves; *Ink:* StazOn, Tsukineko; *Font:* Century Gothic; *Adhesive:* Glue Dots International and Scrapbook Adhesives by 3L; *Other:* Thread.

chicago
TRAINS
I love Chicago. It is one of my favorite cities. Amy and I were there to work, but even so, I was looking forward to spending some time with my good friend away from the daily grind of being a mom.
We took the train down rather than driving and once we got to Union Station we needed to hop on the El to get out to Rosemont. I was pretty excited because I'd never taken the El (or any other city train system) before. I kept thinking of the movie "While You Were Sleeping." We missed the first train trying to figure out what ticket we needed, but once we were on the next one our ride was nice. After our stay in Rosemont our ride on the El back to Union Station wasn't quite so smooth. The normally 30 minute commute took an hour and a half because of track work! The trip included riding the El for a bit, getting off the El and onto a bus for a while and then back onto the El. Amy and I had to literally run several blocks, dragging our luggage behind us, to catch our train at Union Station. Anyway, we made it to our train and the ride home was on time and smooth. I have to say though, as fun as the trains were and umm, were not... next time I'm going to drive. But on the bright side, at least I had my good friend Amy with me!
QUINCY 220S 200W
OUT

Chicago Trains *by Cindy Tobey.* **Supplies** *Cardstock:* Bazzill Basics Paper; *Patterned paper:* Love, Elsie for KI Memories (blue with brown dots) and Scenic Route (all others); *Stickers:* EK Success (label) and Heidi Swapp for Advantus (block letters); *Foam letters:* American Crafts; *Chipboard:* Fancy Pants Designs; *Ribbon:* Michaels (brown stripe) and Pebbles Inc. (red); *Brads:* Making Memories (flower) and Queen & Co. (other); *Buttons:* My Mind's Eye; *Journaling spot and paint:* Making Memories; *Ink:* Tsukineko; *Pen:* Pigma Micron, Sakura; *Font:* Arial Narrow; *Other:* Inkjet label and thread.

OK, this is one cool cityscape! To create this adorable skyline, Cindy cut building shapes from cardstock and backed the window cut-outs with paper and ribbon scraps. The irregular machine-stitched outlines add a charming finishing touch.

22 Come up with a new use for ribbon.

My name is Elizabeth, and I'm a ribbon addict. There—I've said it. If I unrolled all the ribbon in my scrapbook stash and laid it end to end, it would probably reach around the world a few times (at least)! I'll bet you can relate. Let's see how we can use one of our favorite supplies in an unusual way. So, go ahead—get out some of those pretty strands and dream up a fresh use for them.

My little daughter Quincey is such a doll-baby! And I'm not biased at all (hee hee). Her little smiles just light up my world, so I wanted this layout to feel like pure joy. What's happier than ruffled ribbon in concentric circles?

Big Smiles by Elizabeth Kartchner. **Supplies** Patterned paper, letters, ribbon, stickers, flowers, buttons and pin: Making Memories; Font: 2Peas Sailboat; Adhesive: Glue Dots International and Scrapbook Adhesives by 3L; Other: Thread.

Try this:

STITCH RUFFLED RIBBON BLOSSOMS

These pretty blooms can add texture and a sense of exuberance to your page. If you don't have access to a sewing machine, you can easily replicate this technique by hand-stitching the flowers to your layout.

1 With a pen or pencil, draw a swirl on your paper where you want to place your first flower.

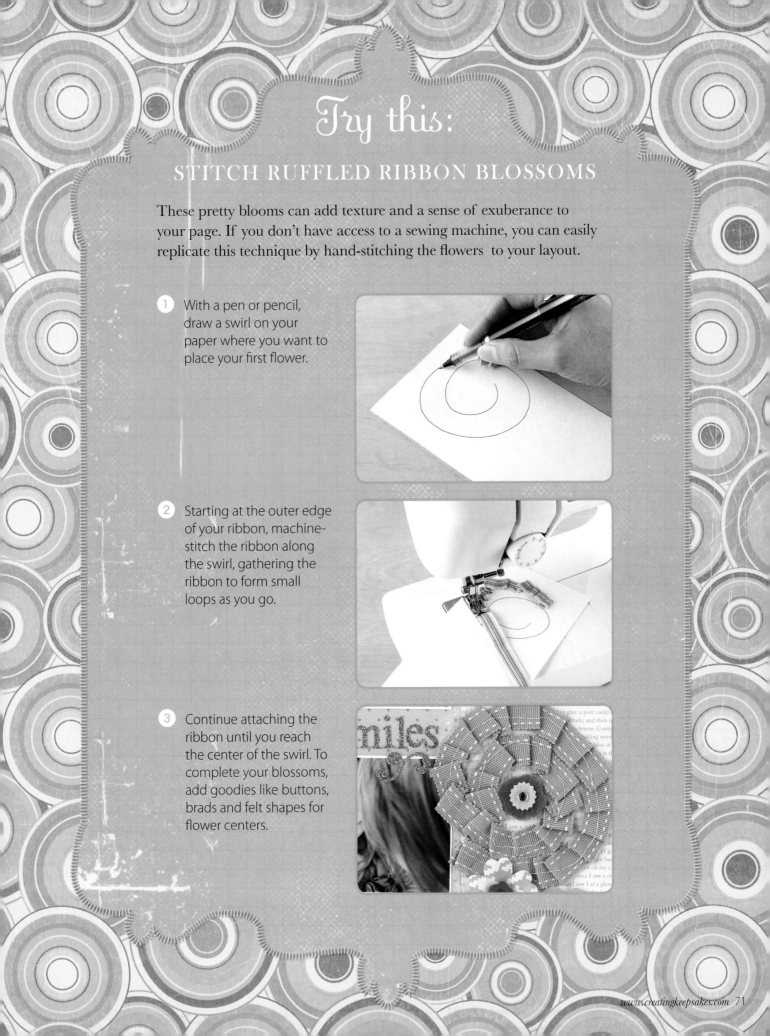

2 Starting at the outer edge of your ribbon, machine-stitch the ribbon along the swirl, gathering the ribbon to form small loops as you go.

3 Continue attaching the ribbon until you reach the center of the swirl. To complete your blossoms, add goodies like buttons, brads and felt shapes for flower centers.

I almost fell over when I saw what Sasha did with ribbon on this page! If I were to tell you there were three different colors of ribbon on this layout, would you be able to locate them? Look closely. First, Sasha punched little circles out of cardstock. Then (here's the genius part) she used glue sealant to attach strips of rickrack to her punched circles. After the sealant was completely dry, she trimmed around the edges and applied another layer of sealant to finish off her circles. Then, she added the handmade accents to her layout. So simple, but totally innovative and cool!

You Are the Smile in My Heart by Sasha Farina. **Supplies** *Cardstock:* Bazzill Basics Paper; *Patterned paper:* Hambly Screen Prints (brown and kraft) and The Scarlet Lime (gray); *Flowers:* Creative Craft Central; *Chipboard letters and accents:* BasicGrey; *Rub-ons:* My Mind's Eye (sentiment) and October Afternoon (brown flowers); *Stickers:* 7gypsies ("Did I ever tell you?"), Hambly Screen Prints (teal circles) and Making Memories (label); *Metal accents and paint:* Making Memories; *Rhinestones:* Prima; *Transparencies:* Hambly Screen Prints; *Gloss medium:* Ranger Industries; *Glue sealant:* Plaid Enterprises; *Other:* Rickrack, buttons and thread.

23 Pair older product with fresh finds for a new look.

I feel sorry for my old supplies sometimes. As I browse through my supplies at home, I get all lightheaded over the pretty, new stuff (excited to dig right in), while the products I've had for some time sit, lonely and neglected, in the back of the drawer. How about showing your old product some love by dusting off some of those perfectly good items and putting them to work again? When combined with more recent purchases, they'll shine like new.

I've had this metal mesh forever. To give it new life, I layered a section of the mesh over rub-ons and stamps, and layered another piece beneath a cut-out opening in my patterned paper. The new silver chipboard stars work perfectly with the metal mesh for a cool, custom look.

PS I Love You *by Elizabeth Kartchner.* **Supplies** *Patterned paper:* Bam Pop, Fancy Pants Designs and Scenic Route; *Rub-ons:* My Mind's Eye; *Metal mesh:* Making Memories; *Stamps:* Hot Off The Press; *Ink:* StazOn, Tsukineko; *Stars:* Heidi Swapp for Advantus; *Font:* American Typewriter; *Adhesive:* Glue Dots International and Scrapbook Adhesives by 3L; *Other:* Eyelets and brads.

Here, Kelly combined old and new products that shared a color scheme. These funky chipboard buttons had been sitting in her stash for two years, just waiting to be used. When she noticed that the new paper she'd selected had similar colors, she immediately mingled the supplies to create this hip layout. Don't be afraid to bring products together that weren't especially designed to "go" with one another—you'll create a refreshing look!

Cake *by Kelly Purkey.* **Supplies** *Cardstock and brads:* American Crafts; *Patterned paper:* American Crafts (pink, yellow, swirl) and KI Memories (teal); *Stickers:* American Crafts (scallops) and BasicGrey (letters); *Decorative scissors and adhesive:* Fiskars Americas; *Chipboard buttons:* Love, Elsie for KI Memories; *Die-cut machine:* Making Memories; *Font:* SP Cake Batter; *Other:* Thread, pen and embroidery floss.

24 Use products from a blind grab into your stash.

Ooh, this challenge is sure to be a fun one! Are you willing to relinquish control? Just close your eyes and reach into your supply drawer or bin or shelf. Pull out the first supplies you grab. OK, open your eyes and work the products onto your next layout. Even if they don't seem to coordinate, you can make it work!

I was a little concerned about the colors of the supplies I'd grabbed for this challenge. (I have to admit that I did end up rejecting a couple of the items because they were so out of keeping with the rest.) I thought to myself, teal, black, brown, white and pink? I finally determined that basing my layout on a neutral background with small touches of color was doable. And you know what? I absolutely love the result! The blind grab forced me outside my typical color choices and opened my eyes to a whole new world.

Hello, Winter *by Elizabeth Kartchner.* **Supplies** *Patterned paper:* October Afternoon (dot) and Sassafras (teal and rose); *Transparency:* Hambly Screen Prints; *Stickers:* American Crafts; *Stamp:* Hot Off The Press; *Ink:* StazOn, Tsukineko; *Brad:* K&Company; *Chipboard:* KI Memories; *Ticket:* Jenni Bowlin Studio; *Adhesive:* Glue Dots International and Scrapbook Adhesives by 3L; *Other:* Pen.

Little a

I love ♥ to watch you study the world At just 2 you see DETAILS I miss and arrive at simple and sometimes BRILLIANT conclusions... like rainbow spiders (fireworks) or coins in my mouth (fillings). I never doubt what you see, I just look more carefully so that I can see

the beautiful WORLD you see

Shelley enthusiastically dug into her scraps for this challenge. Like me, she ended up with a wide variety of papers and had to blend them together onto one layout. Her strategy? She cut the various papers into butterfly shapes and circles, and chose a whimsical, cheerful theme for her layout. Try it yourself! Using random scraps saves money and results in cool pages you may not normally coordinate otherwise.

The Beautiful World You See by Shelley Aldrich. **Supplies** *Patterned paper:* BasicGrey (green paisley and green dot), My Mind's Eye (green, orange, blue dot and yellow dot), Pink Paislee (green grid), Sassafras (yellow dot, heart and blue stripe) and Scenic Route (beige dot, black dot, red dot and gray squares); *Chipboard butterfly:* Scenic Route; *Ink:* ColorBox, Clearsnap; *Embroidery floss:* DMC; *Circle punch:* EK Success; *Colored pencils:* Prismacolor, Sanford; *Pen:* Zig Writer, EK Success.

Try this:

CREATE COLORFUL INKED BUTTERFLIES

These gorgeous accents can be used on a variety of projects, as they'll look different each time, depending on the papers you select. Go beyond butterflies, too—what other chipboard shapes can you put to use as templates?

1 Trace around a chipboard butterfly on the back of a piece of patterned paper to create an outline. Cut out the butterfly shape. Repeat with a smaller chipboard butterfly.

2 Ink the edges of the hand-cut butterflies using an inkpad.

3 Layer the smaller butterfly atop the larger one and attach to page. Use a paper piercer to create a "flight path" on your background paper.

25 Use a page protector as part of your design.

So, we all have functional supplies like page protectors that are meant to be just useful, right? Not so fast! Take that utilitarian page protector and see what you can do with it, and you'll never underestimate your products again.

To meet this challenge, I chose a page protector that was meant to hold film negatives; filled the pockets with photos, paper and embellishments; and then attached it to a fun background paper. Be sure to add curved touches like the journaling spot and the flowers to break up the lines of the page protector. If you like, sew along each row for added detail.

Newport Beach *by Elizabeth Kartchner.* **Supplies** *Patterned paper:* Cosmo Cricket and Scenic Route; *Rub-ons:* American Crafts; *Chipboard:* Scenic Route; *Layered button flower:* Evalicious; *Ticket:* Jenni Bowlin Studio; *Sticker:* Little Yellow Bicycle; *Adhesive:* Glue Dots International and Scrapbook Adhesives by 3L; *Other:* Thread and pen.

TIS

THE SEASON

2008

7 13

81 2 17 27

How amazing is Amanda's page? She created the background, slipped it into a 12" x 12" page protector, machine-stitched around the perimeter, and trimmed the edges. Then, she created pockets to allow the photos and tag to be pulled out. Her journaling, which is on the back of the pockets, can now be read without taking the page out of the protector. So cool!

Tis the Season by Amanda Johnson. **Supplies** *Cardstock:* Archiver's; *Patterned paper:* Hambly Screen Prints (woodgrain), October Afternoon (black and white) and Sassafras (green numbers); *Vinyl stickers:* Headline; *Rub-ons:* Hambly Screen Prints; *Embroidery floss:* DMC; *Font:* Rough Typewriter; *Other:* Thread and label.

26 Incorporate product packaging on a page.

Manufacturers spend lots of money on the design of their packaging to increase their appeal to us consumers. So why let the "throwaway" parts of the everyday products you purchase go to waste? Let's see how creatively you can include product packaging on your next project.

My jaw dropped when I saw Kelly's page! After she'd used all the cute chipboard hearts on other projects, she incorporated the leftover chipboard backing on this page to create a fresh, unusual focal-point accent to go with her layout's theme. She used foam tape to raise the chipboard, allowing her to embellish and add paper beneath it. Now that's a clever use of product packaging!

My 2008 Love List *by Kelly Purkey.*
Supplies *Chipboard packaging:* Heidi Grace Designs; *Cardstock, ribbon, photo corners and buttons:* American Crafts; *Patterned paper:* American Crafts (green scribble and blue), BasicGrey (green floral) and Heidi Grace Designs (diamonds and flowers); *Letter stickers:* Doodlebug Design; *Epoxy sticker:* Cloud 9 Design; *Corner-rounder punch and adhesive:* Fiskars Americas; *Font:* SP Strut; *Other:* Thread.

I nearly got carried away with this challenge. When I started looking at the packaging of my supplies, I was astonished to realize how much cool stuff I had been tossing into the garbage. So my page uses product packaging almost exclusively. Way fun, and cost-effective, too!

New Adventure by Elizabeth Kartchner. **Supplies** Product packaging: American Crafts (letter-stickers background), Autumn Leaves (stamp-holder background), Jenni Bowlin Studio (star trim from Chalkboard letter stickers) and Making Memories (stripe and dot); Hole-punch accents: Random packaging; Font: American Typewriter.

Quiz:
What's in your stash?

I take stock of my stash every six months, and it's really liberating for me. By sorting through all my supplies, I become reacquainted with what's on hand and force myself to be honest about what I actually need and will use. In this quiz, I'd like you to assess your stockpile so you can get more mileage out of what you have.

How do we score this quiz? Well, let's just gauge your success on how well you follow through on the action items you've identified here. Clear out things you don't use, and come up with a plan of attack for maximizing what you've got. In the end, if you're happy, you've passed with flying colors!

1 On the lines below, list three supplies in your stash that you haven't used in a while.

_____

_____

_____

2 Now, try to brainstorm ideas for incorporating those older products into an upcoming project. Write your concepts below. If you can't come up with a viable use for the products, consider passing them on to someone who might enjoy them.

_____

_____

_____

3 On the lines below, list three supplies that you have in abundance.

_____

_____

_____

4 How can you use those tried-and-true products you've amassed in a new way? List some ideas below.

_____

_____

_____

5 What supplies could you combine to achieve a fun, new effect? Write your thoughts here.

_____

_____

_____

LIZZY'S LAST WORD:

Stash suggestions

There are certain products we scrapbookers seem to keep accumulating. For some reason, I'm a sucker for particular types of supplies, and I'm always looking for cool, new contexts for these favorites. I currently have a whole lot of brads, buttons, ribbon, alphabets and stamps, and I'm determined to continue my love affair with them without falling into a creative rut. So without further ado, I present alternate uses for these stash stars.

- **BRADS.** Try using them in between sentences in a journaling block.

- **RIBBON.** Weave a few different pieces together to make a cool background in place of patterned paper.

- **BUTTONS.** Make a covered button. Cut a small square of fabric, wrap the fabric around the button and adhere to the back with liquid adhesive. Hot glue works great.

- **ALPHABETS.** Use numbers from alphabet sets to number journaling strips and lists.

- **STAMPS.** Clear-emboss a stamped image on white paper, then use a spray ink like Glimmer Mist to color the paper. The embossed image will remain white.

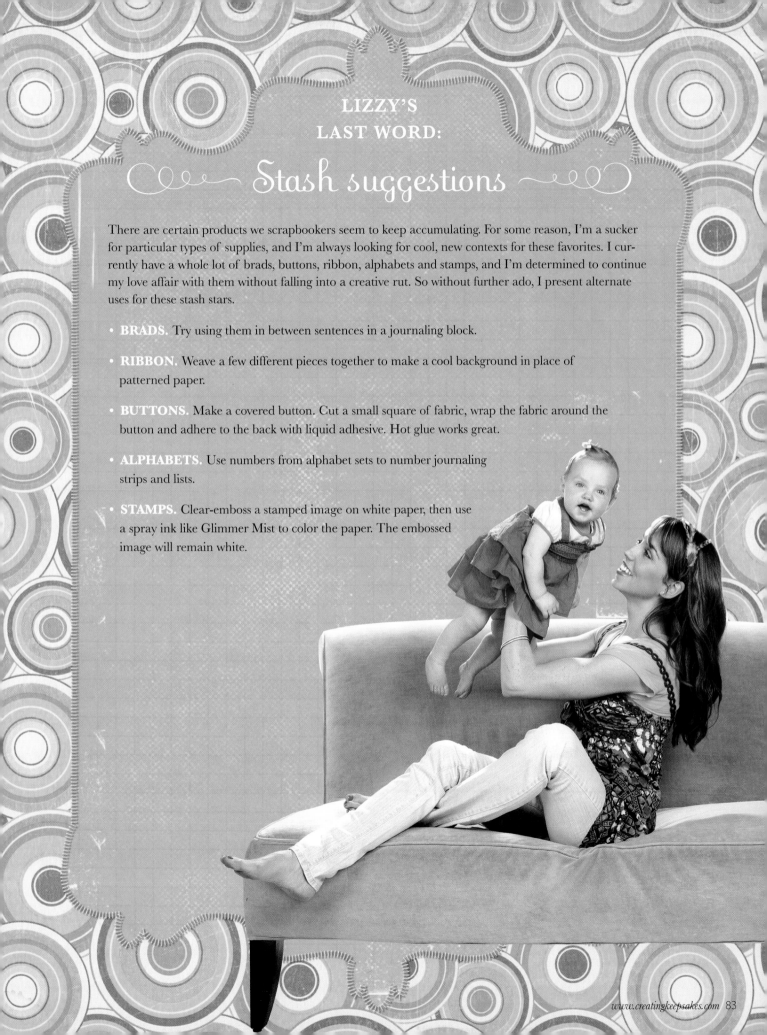

around the house

Scrapbooking's not a new hobby. It's been around for hundreds of years. Before the days of scrapbook stores and online shopping, people decorated their albums with little tidbits of memorabilia from their lives. Let's give our pages the same kind of down-home treatment with the challenges in this chapter.

27 Add commercial print items to a page.

I'm sure you have catalogs or brochures or pamphlets lying around your place. Many of them contain ready-made, gorgeous visuals and photographs. Why not use one on your next layout?

Amanda didn't stop at simply nabbing nice patterns from a paper catalog; she also incorporated the torn spiral fringe for some super-cool texture. I love how she layered paint and her title over pages with type on them for added graphic interest. Oh, and did you notice the stunning photos on her layout? That's really her house!

A House to Call Home *by Amanda Johnson.* **Supplies** *Cardstock:* Archiver's; *Gel pen:* Uni-ball, Newell Rubbermaid; *Other:* Catalog clippings, letter stickers, spray paint and thread.

Licked Clean by Elizabeth Kartchner.
Supplies *Cardstock:* Bazzill Basics Paper; *Patterned paper:* Making Memories; *Letter stickers:* American Crafts; *Transparency:* Hambly Screen Prints; *Butterfly punch:* Martha Stewart Crafts; *Other:* Menu, staples, tag and pen.

Our family loves eating out and ordering in, so we've got lots of menus on hand that we pull out whenever we're feeling hungry. On this layout I combined photos from an outing with clippings from the actual menu. Do you see them? I even used a butterfly punch on sections of the menu to create some unusual accents.

True Love *by Keisha Campbell.* **Supplies** *Cardstock:* Bazzill Basics Paper; *Patterned paper:* Collage Press (ledger) and Making Memories (dot floral); *Ribbon, flower and button:* Making Memories; *Stamps:* Hero Arts, Making Memories and Stampin' Up!; *Adhesive badge:* American Crafts; *Punches:* EK Success and Stampin' Up!; *Other:* Tags, metal clip, card and straight pin.

28 Include a note or greeting card.

Traditional scrapbooks often housed messages from loved ones. I believe it's a practice we should continue. So for this challenge, slip in a letter, a note or a card—just think how special it will be to happen upon it when you pull out your album years from now!

Looking for a unique way to include some personalized, hidden journaling? Try a card with a blank interior. Keisha chose this gorgeous note card to write a special message to her daughters. It adds visually to the layout while performing an important communication function at the same time.

Good Morning Sweetiecakes! Hope you slept ok and had no nightm bad dreams! I dreamed I had a wonderful life with the most beautiful wife in the world... but then I realized, I wasn't dreaming!!! I love you! Have a smooth day!

comfy Love

Comfy Love *by Elizabeth Kartchner.* **Supplies** *Patterned paper:* Fancy Pants Designs and Sassafras; *Letters, adhesive badge and clear sticker:* American Crafts; *Transparency:* Hambly Screen Prints; *Rub-ons:* BasicGrey; *Adhesive:* Glue Dots International and Scrapbook Adhesives by 3L; *Other:* Embroidery floss.

I highly recommend using a note from a loved one as journaling on a layout, even if it's a few years old. This note from my husband was written years ago, but I still wanted to showcase it on my layout and not have it lost in a box somewhere. It provides the perfect complement to these cherished photos of us together.

29 Make use of fabric scraps in your scrapbooking.

I've really fallen in love with fabric. Nothing makes me happier than picking up sumptuous remnants from the craft store. So let's put some on a page. If you don't share my obsession, you can always snip some scraps from an old garment to add a homespun touch to your next project.

The fabric pieces really add warmth to Cindy's page, don't you agree? And though the flowers express a bit of whimsy, their color retains the feeling of the layout's theme. In bright hues, they'd be perfect on a more carefree page, too. Did you notice her fabric "grass" near the bottom of the layout? So charming!

Gloomy by Cindy Tobey. **Supplies** *Cardstock:* Bazzill Basics Paper; *Patterned paper:* Making Memories; *Fabric:* Amy Butler (green circles); *Chipboard:* BasicGrey (letters) and Fancy Pants Designs (leaves); *Buttons:* My Mind's Eye (light blue); *Stamps:* Sassafras; *Ink:* Clearsnap and Stampin' Up!; *Colored pencil:* Newell Rubbermaid; *Pen:* Sakura; *Paint:* Making Memories; *Font:* Century Gothic; *Other:* Felt, fabric (blue and green), embroidery floss, buttons (dark blue), pinking shears and thread.

Try this:

CONSTRUCT FABRIC FLOWERS

You can re-create Cindy's flowers easily. Just follow these simple steps, and your page will blossom in no time.

1 Punch a circle out of cardstock. (Cindy's were 1¼".) Cut a strip of fabric (1" wide for the smaller flower or 1½" wide for the larger one) with pinking shears.

2 Hand-stitch the fabric strip to the cardstock circle, gathering the fabric in pleats as you continue around the circle.

3 Attach felt and buttons with embroidery floss. Be sure to run the floss through the buttonholes and all layers to hold the flower together.

This is seriously one of my favorite pages ever. The sweet picture always gets to me, and I really love how the fabric butterflies turned out. They're really easy to make—just cut out a shape from fabric, pin it down onto paper and then sew around the edges. You can achieve a thousand different looks, depending on the shape and the fabric you choose.

e & c *by Elizabeth Kartchner.* **Supplies** *Patterned paper:* American Crafts (scallop), Heidi Swapp for Advantus (black dot and houndstooth), Jenni Bowlin Studio (cream and music notes), KI Memories (small dot) and Prima (blue grid); *Foam heart and adhesive badge:* American Crafts; *Rub-on:* Jenni Bowlin Studio; *Digital frame (journaling spot):* Skinny Label + Paper by Jennifer Pebbles; *Fabric:* Amy Butler and Michael Miller; *Pin:* Heidi Grace Designs; *Font:* American Typewriter; *Adhesive:* Glue Dots International and Scrapbook Adhesives by 3L; *Other:* Tag, rhinestones, thread, ink, letter stamps and spray ink.

30 Stamp with something other than a stamp.

OK, stay with me. You can do this! Countless objects can be called into use as stamps. Start scoping out the items in your house for something you can use to make a stamped impression. Time to play!

On this layout, Sasha used some torn corrugated cardboard to add interesting lines to her title. Potential stamp materials are everywhere! They're usually hiding in plain sight; you just have to look at things in a different way.

Small, Big, Bigger by Sasha Farina. **Supplies** *Cardstock:* Bazzill Basics Paper. *Patterned paper:* October Afternoon (green), Sassafras (flower and scallop grid) and Scenic Route (grid). *Flowers:* American Crafts (orange and brown felt), Making Memories (green felt) and Prima (blue); *Chipboard accents:* Fancy Pants Designs; *Rub-ons:* Cosmo Cricket; *Transparency:* Hambly Screen Prints; *Rhinestones:* Heidi Swapp for Advantus; *Brads:* BasicGrey (pink) and Making Memories (glitter green); *Stamp:* FontWerks; *Paint:* Making Memories; *Ink:* VersaMark, Tsukineko; *Font:* Teletype (title) and Century Gothic (journaling); *Other:* Buttons, thread and corrugated cardboard.

74

He loves **you!**

When I created this layout, I actually raided my scrapbook supplies for an unusual stamp idea. With a foam brush, I painted the petals of a silk flower, then stamped it onto paper and pressed down each petal to imprint onto my page. I was super excited with how it turned out. It's so easy. Grab something and start stamping!

He Loves You by Elizabeth Kartchner. **Supplies** *Patterned paper:* BasicGrey, Jenni Bowlin Studio and Sassafras; *Transparency and rub-ons:* Hambly Screen Prints; *Letter stickers:* KI Memories; *Stamps:* Hot Off The Press; *Ink:* StazOn, Tsukineko; *Rhinestone swirl:* Glitz Design; *Flower die cut:* My Mind's Eye; *Metal charm, buttons and pin:* Making Memories; *Other:* Silk flower, paint, tag and pen.

31 Incorporate book pages or sheet music on a layout.

Why limit yourself to using scrapbook paper on your projects? I really love the vintage look that book or music papers can add to a page. For this challenge, raid the piano bench or the bookshelf and see what strikes your fancy!

On many occasions, I've had people come up to me and ask, "is she always so happy?" The answer is "yes." Aside from the occasional bad day, which we all have, and the occasional toddler tantrum, you are, without a doubt, an extremely happy little girl. It really doesn't take much to bring that sweet smile to your face either. Big, fancy toys don't impress you much. You're simply overjoyed by the many little things that the rest of us tend to take for granted...butterflies, birdies, floating bubbles, a big red balloon, or finding that perfect rock. I feel so blessed and fortunate to be invited into your world on a daily basis. A world full of sweetness and laughter, sunshine & lollipops. Some days it's just what I need to help put everything back into perspective. I always leave feeling renewed and refreshed, and with a positive outlook. If you're open to it, there truly is a lot you can learn from a four year old.

sunshine and lollipops

Have you ever purchased something not because you needed it, but because it was just too darn cute to pass up? That's what happened to Sheri with the adorable journal whose bird-print cover is featured on her page. Since the chipboard cover was originally quite thick, she thinned it out by carefully peeling off several of the back layers. Because of the bold colors and patterns on the notebook cover, she kept the rest of her design very clean.

Sunshine and Lollipops by Sheri Reguly. **Supplies** *Cardstock:* Bazzill Basics Paper; *Patterned paper:* Bo-Bunny Press; *Flower:* Making Memories; *Button:* SEI; *Brads:* Die Cuts With a View; *Circle punch:* Marvy Uchida; *Journal:* Ecojot; *Thread:* South Maid; *Software:* Microsoft Picture It! Vol. 9; *Fonts:* Fling (title) and Times New Roman (journaling).

Our family reading time is so special to me, I wanted to include book pages on my layout about our ritual. I punched circles from the antique pages to use as decorative elements. And look how cute the chipboard woodland creatures look paired with the book pages! Oh, and a little side tip for you: Try writing your journaling on the white space on a photo (like the arm of the chair in my pictures). Fun, right?

I've been wanting to capture this moment of my two girls sitting on my lap reading books for a while now but Collin was never here to take a photo and if he was Avery suddenly wouldn't want to read a book anymore.

Luckily today my camera was sitting on my desk so I quickly turned it to timer and a couple beeps later these images were taken. Crap, now I have no excuse:).

EVeRydaY

Every Day *by Elizabeth Kartchner.* **Supplies** *Patterned paper:* Crate Paper and Sassafras; *Letters:* Jenni Bowlin Studio; *Chipboard:* Sassafras; *Border sticker:* BasicGrey; *Font:* 2Peas Tubby; *Adhesive:* Glue Dots International and Scrapbook Adhesives by 3L; *Other:* Circle punches (scalloped and regular), date stamp and ink.

32 Design a layout using children's artwork.

Before we know it, our little ones will be bigger ones. We can't stop them from growing up, but we can preserve pieces of their childhood in our albums. For this challenge, feature your little Picasso's masterpiece on a page.

you color my world.

When I'm in my scraproom designing a project, Avery loves to work on her own little creations. After she finished splashing some watercolors on the text paper, I penciled some leaf shapes on my layout, cut them out with a craft knife and placed her painting behind the openings. Touches of her art show through and give a glimpse without overwhelming the page.

Color My World *by Elizabeth Kartchner.* **Supplies** *Cardstock:* Bazzill Basics Paper; *Patterned paper:* BasicGrey (yellow), KI Memories (stripe) and October Afternoon (text); *Rub-ons:* American Crafts; *Other:* Watercolors and thread.

Your favorite character
is Angelina Ballerina.
We watch her TV shows, DVDs
and   read her books.
                You say that
         you   want to be a ballerina
when you grow up.

                    Ever so often, I catch you
swirling around   the house   in your pink tutu,
pirouetting up and   down the stairs and tippy-toeing around us
                     humming some sweet tune.

                        I don't know
                        if you will really
become a ballerina some day, but when you   get the choice to
                            sit it out

or dance,

I hope
you
dance!

always

While my layout showed small glimpses of Avery's artwork, Mou's showcases her daughter's drawing front and center. Mou cut around the drawing, glued it to her page, painted an outline around it and sewed on an adorable tutu with pink crepe paper. Her photos, title, journaling and accents were all built around the artwork. Stunning!

I Hope You Dance by Mou Saha. **Supplies**
Cardstock: Frances Meyer; *Paint:* Delta Creative; *Rhinestones:* Rusty Pickle; *Embroidery floss:* DMC; *Pen:* American Crafts; *Other:* Crepe paper.

Try this:

CREATE CREPE-PAPER RUFFLES

Whether you want to create a skirt, like Mou did, or simply add a ruffle to your page, you'll love this technique.

① Lay down an arc of adhesive where you want the ruffle to be. Pleat and adhere the crepe paper as you go.

② Poke holes in a line across the top of the ruffle and hand-stitch through the holes to attach the ruffle.

③ Adhere ruffle to your page.

SNL, Stand-By Style by Kelly Purkey. **Supplies** *Cardstock, rub-ons and brads:* American Crafts; *Patterned paper:* American Crafts (green and squares), Cosmo Cricket (red) and KI Memories (blue); *Letter stickers:* BasicGrey; *Decorative scissors, punches and adhesive:* Fiskars Americas; *Font:* AL Old Remington; *Other:* Thread and ticket.

33 Include memorabilia.

This challenge brings back old-school scrapbooking. Dig up that souvenir you've kept in a drawer or envelope and put it to work as a page embellishment. What better way to remember a trip or event than an actual piece of history from that time?

Kelly's stand-by ticket from *Saturday Night Live* was a great souvenir from a New York City trip that she wanted to display on a page instead of keep hidden away. She framed it by creating a grid out of squares that matched the patterned-paper background. It's part of her design, not just an afterthought. Love that!

Lunch with Mary *by Elizabeth Kartchner.* **Supplies** *Cardstock:* Bazzill Basics Paper; *Patterned paper, letters, ribbon and pen:* American Crafts; *Transparency:* Hambly Screen Prints; *Rub-ons:* American Crafts and Hambly Screen Prints; *Journaling spot:* KI Memories; *Other:* Buttons, negative and scallop square punch.

I took a slightly different approach to this challenge. My souvenir isn't of this particular lunch date but of an era in general. Since I've gone digital with my photography, I don't actually get film negatives of my shots any more, but since we always take so many pictures when we're together, an old negative seemed like a cool accent. Add rub-ons and ribbons for a totally delightful result!

34 Free for all! Use something random from around the house.

I got so excited when I began to look around the house, because I discovered that there was a ton of potential scrapbook product right in front of my nose. So this challenge is wide open. Grab something and add it to your next page.

Oh, how Avery loves watching the Disney Channel. She becomes totally absorbed—it's so cute. The Disney clothing tag was too perfect for this layout. Paired with the quirky frame and other funny accents, it was tailor-made for this page about Avery in the land of princesses—her version of heaven on earth!

The Daze by Elizabeth Kartchner.
Supplies *Patterned paper:* Making Memories, Sassafras and SEI; *Letters and stickers:* American Crafts; *Chipboard:* KI Memories; *Adhesive:* Glue Dots International and Scrapbook Adhesives by 3L; *Other:* Tag, pen and brads.

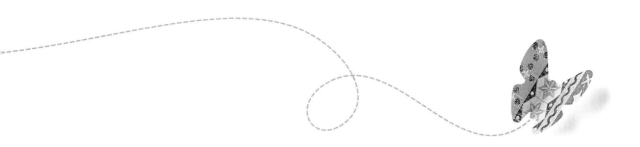

my life is much more *colorful* ...just because of the things you say daily

Keisha chose a magazine page for her layout. Why not? It had a ready-made title, and the gorgeous butterflies added eye candy and thematic support for her layout. Keep your eyes open for the possibilities the next time you're enjoying your favorite periodical.

In Love with Color by Keisha Campbell.
Supplies *Cardstock:* BasicGrey and Bazzill Basics Paper; *Patterned paper, phrase stickers and button:* Making Memories; *Punches:* Marvy Uchida (flowers and tag); *Font:* Splendid 66; *Other:* Magazine page, chipboard (brackets and scallop), date stamp, ink and stick pin.

Quiz:

Are you acid-free?

I took up scrapbooking for artistic reasons, but I also want my creations to last. Let's see what we know about keeping our projects archival-quality.

Compare your answers with the following:

Mostly A's: You are honored to document important memories. However, some of your habits may be shortening the life of your photos. I was right here not too long ago! Yellowed, brittle pictures and papers indicate deterioration. *Action plan: Remove photos from magnetic albums, and store your scrapbooks upright (to prevent weakening the bindings).*

Mostly B's: You believe your photos must be shared, so your decisions are all about interaction. That's very commendable! Unfortunately, exposure to light and the oils on human hands can be detrimental to your heirlooms. *Action plan: Use acid-free page protectors and keep a bookshelf in the room where you entertain so guests and family members can enjoy your albums.*

Mostly C's: You're very aware of archival practices and understand that your photos are precious. Way to go! *Action plan: Share your knowledge with fellow scrapbookers at your next crop.*

Mostly D's: You're a funny one! Collin, is this you? *Action plan: Um, I think you may be beyond help. Just kidding! Though you'd be amusing to hang around with!*

---

1 Which of the following causes deterioration of photos and heirloom objects?

  A Exposure to moisture and pollution.

  B Exposure to light and heat.

  C Both A and B.

  D Talking on the cell phone while driving.

2 What is the safest method for storing scrapbook albums?

  A Stack them atop one another.

  B Prop them open, so people can peruse them.

  C Line them up on a bookshelf.

  D Hide them in a vault underground, guarded by a big, snarling dog.

3 What is the safest plan regarding your photos?

  A Store them in a magnetic photo album.

  B Keep them easily accessible so others can enjoy them.

  C Use doubles and store the originals in an acid-free box in a cool, dark, dry place.

  D Hang them on the clothesline with colorful clothespins.

4 What is the best way to include an heirloom document in your albums?

  A Attach it right to the page with scrapbooking adhesive.

  B Create a pocket on your layout so it can be pulled out and shared.

  C Make a photocopy or scan it, and keep the original in a safe place.

  D Crunch it up and attach it to your layout as a dimensional accent.

5 What can you do to treat paper items that may not be acid-free if you want to display them in your albums?

  A What's acid-free, again?

  B You can't treat them. If you want people to interact with them, it's a sacrifice you must make.

  C Spray them with a deacidification product, like Archival Mist.

  D Crush an antacid tablet like Tums or Alka-Seltzer on them.

LIZZY'S LAST WORD:

Scavenger hunt

Here's a fun little exercise for you. Go on a 30-minute scavenger hunt around your house and search for 10 items you could use on a layout. You'll be amazed how easy it is to come up with cool things to implement in your scrapbooking. Here are some items I found and a few ideas about how you can use each item on your next page:

- **RECEIPTS.** What about including them in a pocket or envelope on a layout? It'll be fun to look back someday and see what you bought and how much it cost.

- **SEASHELLS.** These are really cool on vacation layouts. Try adding some rhinestones to give them extra punch.

- **AN ORANGE.** I told you potential stamping materials are everywhere! Go ahead and slice one in half, paint it and stamp onto a page.

- **A COLORING BOOK.** Ah, ready-made evidence of your child's creativity. Put a few pages to work as the background for a layout.

- **TICKETS.** If you're like me, you've got quite a few mementos from sporting events and concerts. Punch them into fun embellishments.

- **PLANT LEAVES.** Flatten a few inside a book. Later, ink them with an inkpad, lay them on a piece of paper, and use a rubber brayer to transfer the leaf image onto a page.

- **HAIR BARRETTE.** This will make a super-adorable accent on a girly page. Just clip it to the edge of a photo or paper.

- **GARMENT TAG.** Many tags already have ribbon or twill attached. Cover part of the tag with a bit of cardstock to make a perfect journaling spot.

- **OLD CLOTHING.** Some things just aren't fit to give to charity. But you could cut strips and tie the fabric to a mini-album binding for a touch of funky fiber.

- **JUNK MAIL.** How about punching letter shapes out of some junk mail for a fun alphabet? What a playful, modern look for your next page!

journaling

I'm a big believer in the power of words. I rarely create a layout without journaling, even if I end up tucking it behind a photo or another element. Sometimes it's a struggle to make it interesting or meaningful or different, but I believe it's worth it to make the effort. Let the challenges in this chapter inspire your inner writer.

35 Formulate a quiz.

Here's a fun idea: Create your journaling in the form of a quiz. Whether it's multiple-choice, true/false or fill-in-the-blank, use a cool, interactive "test" approach to convey your information.

Quincey update

baby girl   3 mos.

Baby's full NAME: _quincey rose_

Baby's NICK NAME:
o q-ball   ✓ q-biscuit
o q-t pie   o Lady q

Baby's LENGTH & WEIGHT
● chubby and round
o tiny and long

HAIR   o Blonde   ✓ Brown   o Baldy   o Red
EYES   ✓ Blue   o Green   o Brown   o Hazel

LOVES TO   ✓ Eat   ✓ Sleep   ✓ Poop   ✓ Smile

Feature most like Mom's
o Nose   o Head
✓ Eyes   o Smile

Feature Most like Dad's
o Nose   o Head
o Eyes   ✓ Smile

BURPS   ✓ some   o and then spits up   o like her Daddy
CRIES   o some   o when hungry   ✓ like her Mommy
GAS   o some   o not much   ✓ like her Daddy
FIRSTS   ✓ cooing   o rolling over   o lifting head   o smiling

Smiles when _you look at her & if her tummy's full_
Favorite Lullaby _"I am like a star..."_
Favorite Activity _laughing as she watches Avery_
Sleeps _a few hours_   Cries _enough_

Is she a:
✓ Night Owl
o Morning Bird
o Both

Things about Quincey we find most enduring:
o Her non stop eating habits
o Her captivating smile
o When she sucks her thumb
✓ All of the above

Extra Credit: _____

The quiz format was just the ticket for this layout about my little Q-Biscuit's characteristics at three months old. Paired with a few representative photos, I now have a great memento of these precious early days with her. Isn't it more interesting than just saying, "Her eyes are blue," or "She has her dad's smile"?

Quincey *by Elizabeth Kartchner.* **Supplies** *Cardstock:* Bazzill Basics Paper; *Patterned paper:* Daisy D's Paper Co.; *Letters:* Making Memories; *Flower:* Prima; *Felt:* Fancy Pants Designs; *Mirror bird:* Heidi Swapp for Advantus; *Fonts:* 2Peas Sailboat and Times New Roman; *Adhesive:* Glues Dots International and Scrapbook Adhesives by 3L; *Other:* Baby card, brads, pen, punches and thread.

What's your favorite color? Blue Pink What's your favorite television show? NHL On The Fly The Backyardigans What's your favorite food? Chicken Bananas,Toast and Cereal What's your favorite movie? Kung Fu Panda Home Alone What's your favorite thing about school? Recess and Math Playing Blocks What do you want to be when you grow up? A Hockey Player A Pirate Arrr! What would you buy with one hundred dollars? Lots Of Candy A Baby What's your favorite game? Head Coach Dora The Explorer What's your favorite sport? Hockey Basketball What's your favorite treat? Bar-B-Q Chips Cake What's your favorite beverage? Root Beer Apple Juice What's your favorite toy? PlayStation Dolls

Sheri quizzed her two children separately so their answers didn't influence one another. Color-coding them pink and blue visually distinguishes their answers. Her sweet little daughter wants to be a pirate! How funny!

He Said, She Said by Sheri Reguly. **Supplies** *Cardstock:* Bazzill Basics Paper; *Patterned paper:* Bo-Bunny Press, Creative Imaginations and October Afternoon; *Letters, flowers and flower brad:* Making Memories; *Metal-rimmed tags:* Hero Arts (small) and Making Memories (large); *Ribbon:* KI Memories; *Paper trim:* Doodlebug Design; *Button:* My Mind's Eye; *Brads:* Bazzill Basics Paper, Die Cuts With a View and Doodlebug Design; *Punches:* EK Success (butterfly) and Marvy Uchida (scallop circle); *Digital element:* Labeled Female Brush Set by Anna Aspnes; *Software:* Adobe Photoshop Elements 6; *Font:* AL Uncle Charles.

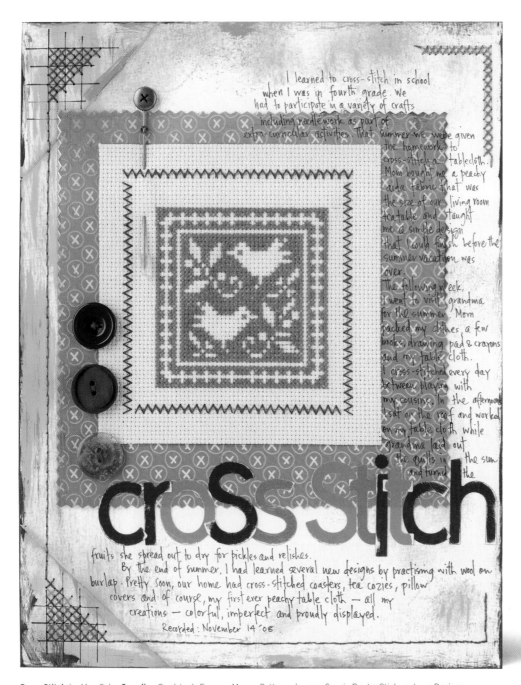

I learned to cross-stitch in school when I was in fourth grade. We had to participate in a variety of crafts including needlework as part of extra-curricular activities. That summer we were given the homework to cross-stitch a tablecloth. Mom bought me a peachy aida fabric that was the size of our living room teatable and taught me a simple design that I could finish before the summer vacation was over.

The following week, I went to visit grandma for the summer. Mom packed my clothes, a few books, drawing pad & crayons and my table cloth. I cross-stitched every day between playing with my cousins. In the afternoons I sat on the roof and worked on my table cloth while grandma laid out the quilts in the sun and turned the

cross stitch

fruits she spread out to dry for pickles and relishes.
By the end of summer, I had learned several new designs by practising with wool on burlap. Pretty soon, our home had cross-stitched coasters, tea cozies, pillow covers and of course, my first ever peachy table cloth — all my creations — colorful, imperfect and proudly displayed.
Recorded: November 14 '06

Cross Stitch *by Mou Saha.* **Supplies** *Cardstock:* Frances Meyer; *Patterned paper:* Scenic Route; *Stickers:* Luxe Designs; *Buttons:* Rusty Pickle; *Paint:* Plaid Enterprises; *Pinking shears:* Fiskars Americas; *Pin:* EK Success; *Embroidery floss:* DMC; *Pen:* American Crafts; *Other:* Cross-stitch fabric, cross-stitch pattern and sandpaper.

36 Base a layout on a memory, even if you don't have a photo for it.

Sometimes there are stories that just need to be told. If an event occurred before you became a scrapbooker, or even if it didn't, you may not have a good picture to go along with your memory. So what? Tell the story anyway.

Mou met the challenge by using a memento as the centerpiece of her page. Every element on this page, from the graph and patterned papers to the buttons and pins, helped her tell her story. Even though the layout has no photo, her page honors a memory that is significant to her.

Try this:

CROSS-STITCH CORNER ACCENTS

Mou's corner design doesn't need to be confined to a page about cross-stitching. It's a folksy decoration that can add a homey touch to any layout. Here's how:

1 Using a ruler or just freehand sketching, draw a grid for the corner cross-stitching. Pierce holes at intersections on the grid.

2 Using the holes as your guide, stitch "x" patterns over the grid.

3 Continue as desired. Erase pencil marks when you are done.

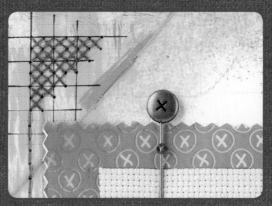

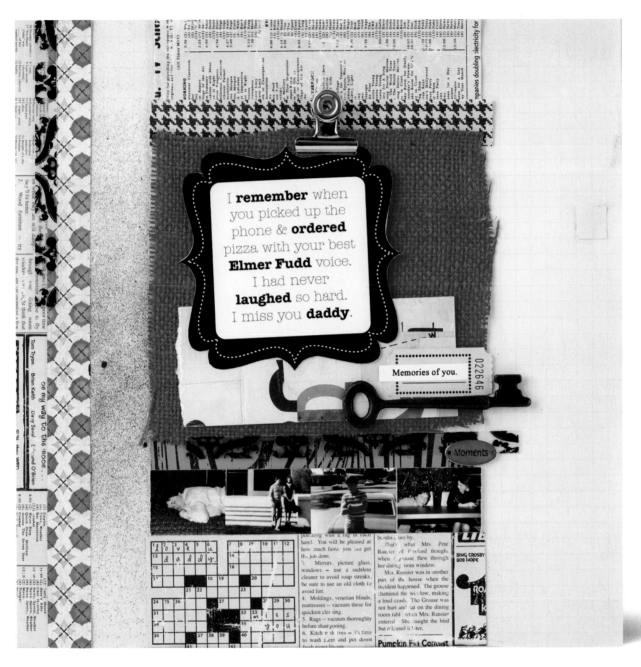

I **remember** when you picked up the phone & **ordered** pizza with your best **Elmer Fudd** voice. I had never **laughed** so hard. I miss you **daddy.**

Memories of you.

Moments

The tiny vintage photographs don't correspond literally with the incident I describe on my layout, but they do help give more insight into my dad's fun personality. Note that I didn't go on for paragraphs. Sometimes it only takes a few representative photos and a few well-chosen words to express yourself meaningfully.

Miss You, Daddy by Elizabeth Kartchner. **Supplies** *Patterned paper:* Daisy D's Paper Co., Hambly Screen Prints, October Afternoon, Sassafras and Scenic Route; *Transparency:* Hambly Screen Prints; *Metal charm:* All My Memories; *Digital frame:* Swank Labels by Jennifer Pebbles; *Adhesive:* Glue Dots International and Scrapbook Adhesives by 3L; *Software:* Adobe Photoshop CS2; *Other:* Fabric, font, key, ticket, clamp and spray ink.

37 Include your journaling within your title.

This time, instead of concerning yourself with the actual content of your text, play with its placement within the design. For this challenge, simply change things up by incorporating your journaling within your title. Have fun!

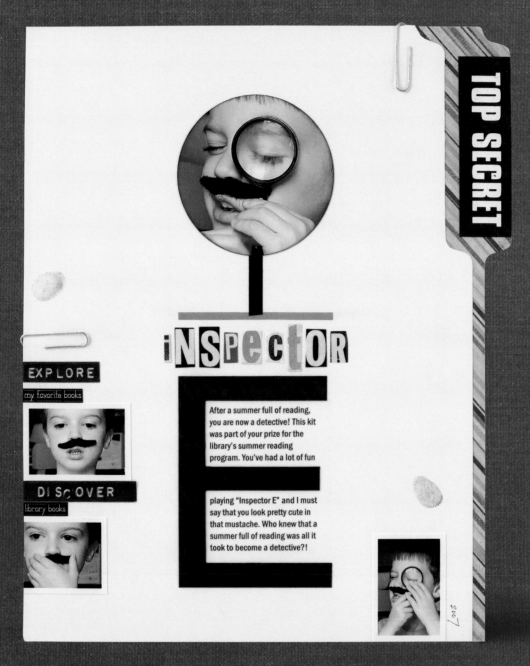

After a summer full of reading, you are now a detective! This kit was part of your prize for the library's summer reading program. You've had a lot of fun

playing "Inspector E" and I must say that you look pretty cute in that mustache. Who knew that a summer full of reading was all it took to become a detective?!

OK, you gotta admit that this is pretty doggone cute. The circular photo in the shape of a magnifying glass, the ransom-note letter treatment and the fingerprints all add up to a clever concept. But Cindy's outside-of-the-box mix of journaling and title gives this layout an extra dose of wow. I suspect you'll want to steal this idea!

Inspector E *by Cindy Tobey.* **Supplies** *Cardstock:* Bazzill Basics Paper; *Patterned paper:* Fancy Pants Designs; *Stickers:* 7gypsies (phrases), K&Company (words) and Rusty Pickle (letters); *Decorative tape:* Heidi Swapp for Advantus (orange); *Ink:* Tsukineko; *Fonts:* Arial (large "E") and Franklin Gothic Medium Condensed (journaling); *Other:* File folder, black decorative tape, paper clips and pen.

If you're anything like me, you just melt when you see newborn babies. To meet this challenge, I wanted a really soft look to fit the topic of the page, so I used an outline font to create a pink letter inside which I could include handwritten journaling. Try this technique for a tender page about your favorite newborn.

Baby Q by Elizabeth Kartchner. **Supplies** Cardstock: Bazzill Basics Paper; *Patterned paper, journaling spot and buttons:* Making Memories; *Rub-ons:* BasicGrey; *Heart accent and adhesive badge:* American Crafts; *Tape and flowers:* Prima; *Adhesive:* Glue Dots International and Scrapbook Adhesives by 3L; *Other:* Pen, punches and rhinestones.

Try this:

CUT A CIRCULAR PHOTO MAT

Add variety to your album with an unusual photo mat. This design was very different for me, but I loved the outcome. Here's how you can make your own cardstock mat for round photos and accent clusters:

1 Determine the size and number of circles you want to use. Mark the center spot for each circle and use a circle cutter to cut them out. (Note: You can also use a cup or other round object as a template and cut out by hand.)

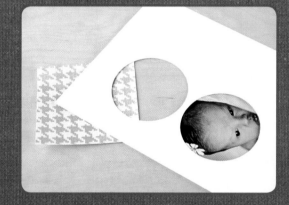

2 Trim and adhere photos behind some circles and paper behind others.

3 Add rub-ons and other embellishments. Layer some across edges of photos and onto mat.

38 Play favorites or explore unique qualities.

It's always fascinating to read about people's favorites or unique characteristics. Journal about someone and the things that make her happy or special. It's guaranteed to make you laugh or smile!

It Was a Very Good Year by Beth Opel. **Supplies** Cardstock: Bazzill Basics Paper; Patterned paper: Bo-Bunny Press (yellow dot), Collage Press (pink floral), Heidi Grace Designs (green plaid), KI Memories (aqua starburst and orange floral), Sandylion (purple flourish), Scenic Route (red) and Tinkering Ink (gray swirl); Epoxy accents: Autumn Leaves (pink butterfly) and SEI (red flower); Transparency: Hambly Screen Prints; Rub-ons: American Crafts (script letters) and SEI (blue flower and dot stem); Letter stickers: American Crafts (white), Doodlebug Design (red) and Heidi Swapp for Advantus (black); Yellow dot flower and paper trim: Doodlebug Design; Felt: Creative Café, EK Success (heart) and Queen & Co. (yellow flower); Rhinestones: Heidi Swapp for Advantus; Adhesive badge and chipboard star: American Crafts; Star label: Jenni Bowlin Studio; Metal dot stickers: Colorbök; Font: Futura Narrow.

After a recent move, Beth began thinking about the stages of her life. She found photos of herself at various ages and then created columns showing where she was living, what she was driving, what music she liked and so on during those times. This layout is also great for a school album or a birthday or just an everyday exercise.

WONDERFUL

SASSY

caring, hostess, gracious
great cook
cry baby
hair dresser
shopper at anthropologie
subscriber to: Martha Stewart
loves to shop

playful, crafty, planner
no time to cook
cry baby
scrapbooker
shopper at Forever 21
subscriber to: Domino
loves to laugh

outgoing, fun, athlete wife
dinner dates
no babies (yet)
student
shopper at J Crew
subscriber to: Fitness mag
loves to exercise

all about us

My sisters and I have so much in common but are quite distinct from each other, too. Exploring our similarities and differences on this layout was a blast! Why not make a page of this kind about your friends or members of your family?

Sisters by Elizabeth Kartchner. **Supplies** *Cardstock, patterned paper and chipboard:* American Crafts; *Rub-ons:* Cosmo Cricket (words) and October Afternoon ("all about us"); *Rhinestones:* Glitz Design; *Chipboard swirl:* Fancy Pants Designs; *Font:* 2Peas Sailboat; *Other:* Paint, thread and tulle.

39 Format your journaling as a Mad Lib.

You know what a Mad Lib is, right? It's a story template where words are left out, allowing you to fill in the blanks with your own answers. The result is always entertaining! Compose your own for a witty alternative to typical journaling.

I wanted this page to really depict a feeling of exhilaration with the tilt and the bright colors, and using a Mad Lib set-up gave the journaling a goofy, perky touch. Bordering the journaling strip with lots of happy photos adds to the joyful vibe.

Pinch Me *by Elizabeth Kartchner.* **Supplies** *Cardstock:* Bazzill Basics Paper; *Patterned paper:* BasicGrey and KI Memories; *Border sticker:* BasicGrey; *Chipboard:* Fancy Pants Designs (swirl) and KI Memories (flowers and butterfly); *Letters:* American Crafts; *Spray ink:* Glimmer Mist, Tattered Angels; *Font:* 2Peas Sailboat; *Other:* Pen.

she's a talkie

Moya would *talk* on the phone all day, everyday if we
name   verb   noun

would let *her*. I actually *think* it is *cute* how *she*
him/her   verb   adjective   he/she

calls *her* *girlfriends* and *talks* forever. It
verb   him/her   noun   verb

reminds me of my *younger* *self*. But don't tell
verb   adjective   noun

her I said that! I'd *never* get to use the *phone*!
him/her   adverb   verb   noun

Premade Mad Libs exist, but like me, Cindy created her own to make it more specific to the story she wanted to tell. Notice how she constructed sentences that highlight the very words that are key to explaining her daughter's fascination with the phone. Instead of filling in the blanks with a pen, she used a handwriting font. Plus, she got to brush up on her parts of speech in the process!

She's a Talkie by Cindy Tobey. **Supplies** *Cardstock:* Bazzill Basics Paper (scallop); *Patterned paper:* American Crafts (speech bubble), Bo-Bunny Press (pink dot), KI Memories (blue stripe) and Scenic Route (green circles); *Rub-on:* Love, Elsie for KI Memories; *Stickers:* American Crafts (letters) and Luxe Designs (epoxy); *Chipboard:* American Crafts; *Ribbon:* Making Memories; *Buttons:* My Mind's Eye; *Fonts:* Arial Narrow and CK Ali's Writing; *Other:* Thread.

40 Represent multiple perspectives.

One way to spice up your journaling is to enlist help. Ask another person for his or her thoughts, and merge them with your own to provide a more complete picture of the event or topic. What a great way to share your memories about the things that matter to you both!

The birth of a baby is an emotional, unforgettable experience for any couple. For this layout, I asked Collin to write down his reaction to Quincey's arrival. His touching words (as well as my own) were very personal and special, so I added journaling pockets by sewing onto the page. We now have a record of how we felt during this important moment. Try this idea for any momentous occasion involving more than one person.

She's Here *by Elizabeth Kartchner.* **Supplies**
Cardstock: Bazzill Basics Paper; *Patterned paper:* American Crafts and K&Company; *Letters:* American Crafts (blue) and Heidi Swapp for Advantus (pink); *Flowers:* Prima; *Brads:* K&Company; *Mini letter stickers:* Making Memories; *Rhinestones:* Glitz Design; *Other:* Chipboard accents, circle punches and thread.

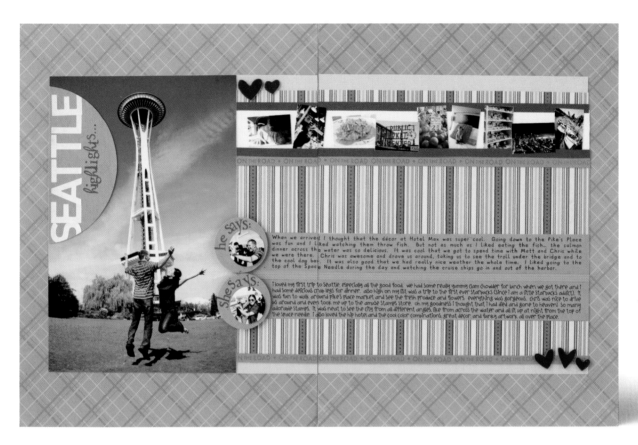

Whenever we get back from a vacation, our family likes to sit around and relive our favorite moments or sights. Kelly took this practice just a little further and listed the most memorable aspects of their Seattle trip from both her boyfriend's viewpoint and her own. Consider this technique for an upcoming project—your layout will have a wider scope if you represent multiple perspectives.

Seattle Highlights *by Kelly Purkey.* **Supplies** *Cardstock:* American Crafts (brown and blue) and Bazzill Basics Paper (kraft); *Patterned paper:* Heidi Grace Designs; *Stamps:* Hero Arts; *Ink:* Stampin' Up!; *Letter stickers:* American Crafts; *Punches:* Fiskars Americas; *Fonts:* BMW Hisba Bahix and SP Miss Patty's; *Other:* Chipboard hearts.

Quiz:
Say what?

What's your journaling type? Choose the letter of the answer that best describes you as it relates to journaling on your layouts.

Answers:

MOSTLY A'S: Journaling seems to be one of the main reasons you enjoy scrapbooking. You like to shake it up and try new things. Hopefully you've been inspired by the challenges in this chapter.

MOSTLY B'S: Photos are the focus in your scrapbooking. Your journaling is based on what's depicted in the photographs, and that's cool. Don't be afraid to stretch a little and take on some of the challenges I've suggested!

MOSTLY C'S: You're all about getting it done. Time is at a premium for you, but you love to create scrapbooks to document your life. Test out a challenge or two from this chapter—several of them are actually real timesavers!

MOSTLY D'S: You like to scrapbook for reasons other than written expression. Maybe you place more emphasis on the art. That's totally OK. But consider trying an idea from this chapter. You never know—you might get hooked!

1 At what point in the layout process do you add journaling?

A I usually start with the journaling and build my layout around it.

B I usually choose photos and then brainstorm what I'd like to say about them.

C I usually add a little journaling at the very end wherever I have some leftover space.

D I usually don't journal.

2 Do you type or handwrite your journaling?

A Some of each.

B Type.

C Handwrite.

D I usually don't journal.

3 How do you format your journaling?

A Lots of different ways.

B In paragraphs or a typical journaling block.

C In captions around my pictures.

D Um, I usually don't journal, remember?

4 What best describes the content of your journaling?

A I try to be meaningful or clever or funny.

B I write about what the photos mean to me.

C I note what's happening in the photos.

D Hello, haven't you been paying attention? I'm not big on journaling.

5 How do you come up with your journaling?

A I prepare it ahead of time or at least think carefully about it before I begin.

B I think hard about it while looking at the photos I want to use.

C I just jot down a few descriptions to identify the people or events for future reference.

D I give up. How do I?

LIZZY'S
LAST WORD:

Just write

To me, journaling is an essential piece of the puzzle—it adds meaning and ties the entire page together. I feel like my pages are incomplete without words to support my photos and describe my thoughts. Even if you don't believe that journaling is your strong suit, I encourage you to express yourself on your pages. You don't have to be a good writer to have something worthwhile to say.

To improve your journaling skills, try these ideas:

- Write journaling on your children's pages as if you're talking to them. I think it adds meaning.

- Free-write before you start composing the journaling for a layout. It helps you dig deeper for something that goes beyond the photos.

- Keep a journal and use excerpts on your layouts, or use a blog post for journaling on a page. Previously written blog posts are the greatest—when I sit down to scrapbook, I already have my journaling ready.

- Involve all of your senses. Bringing in details of sounds, smells, tastes and the like will make your writing more appealing.

Check out these suggestions for varying your journaling approach:

- Hide it behind a photo or page element.

- Cut journaling into word strips.

- Digitally add journaling to your photo before you print.

- Write directly onto your photo with a pen.

- Journal inside a circle or other shape.

- Angle your journaling.

- Incorporate a funny quote.

techniques

One of the things I love most about scrapbooking is the opportunity to play and experiment. I'm always looking for new techniques to add zing to my pages. This chapter is packed full of fabulous must-try ways to get your craft on!

41 Use shape die cuts creatively.

I seem to be reaching for my die-cut machine more and more these days. Playing with shapes is just so fun! If you don't have a machine, do something unusual with punches or premade die cuts for this challenge.

Sometimes a certain shape can really help you tell the story on your layout. I cut raindrops in various sizes out of cardstock and photos to convey Avery's cheerful, "singin' in the rain" mood. The result? A happy, high-energy page that captures the moment just perfectly.

Fabulous Forecast by Elizabeth Kartchner. **Supplies** *Cardstock:* Bazzill Basics Paper and Wausau Paper; *Patterned paper:* Making Memories; *Letters:* American Crafts; *Cloud die cut:* Cosmo Cricket; *Die-cut machine:* Cricket, Provo Craft; *Font:* 2Peas Tubby; *Other:* Thread.

How clever is this? Cindy used various hand punches to create her own shape die cuts out of a Krispy Kreme pastry bag! Some thin materials don't work well with hand punches because the paper is too flexible. To solve this problem, simply thicken the material by securing it to a sheet of paper with removable adhesive. Punch your shapes and peel the paper off.

Donuts with Daddy *by Cindy Tobey.* **Supplies**
Patterned paper: BasicGrey (brown stripe), Cosmo Cricket (green and red) and Karen Foster Design (ruled); *Letters:* BasicGrey (green) and Doodlebug Design (red sticker and red chipboard); *Ribbon:* Crate Paper; *Brads:* Queen & Co.; *Button:* Rusty Pickle; *Ink:* Clearsnap; *Punches:* EK Success (flower and scalloped circles) and Martha Stewart for EK Success (butterfly); *Circle cutter:* Creative Memories; *Pen:* Sakura; *Font:* Century Gothic; *Other:* Pastry bag.

42 Build your own page embellishments.

Get more mileage from your supplies by learning new ways to use them. For this challenge, layer products for a terrific look. It's a fresh, easy trick!

That Kelly! She's the queen of dimensional accents.
For this page, she created really fun embellishments with punches, stamps and cardstock. Copy her technique for color-coordinated decorations you can make with supplies you already have.

New Yorkers by Kelly Purkey. **Supplies** Cardstock: American Crafts (green, purple and pink) and Bazzill Basics Paper (kraft); Patterned paper: Heidi Grace Designs; Stamps: Hero Arts; Ink: Stampin' Up!; Punches, foam stamps and decorative-edged scissors: Fiskars Americas; Letters: American Crafts; Epoxy stickers: Cloud 9 Design; Font: SP Strut; Other: Thread.

Try this:

CRAFT DIMENSIONAL STAMPED ACCENTS

Give your pages a little vertical interest with dimensional stamped accents. Kelly used a butterfly stamp, but you can try this idea with any number of stamps.

1 Stamp the butterfly on two different colors of cardstock.

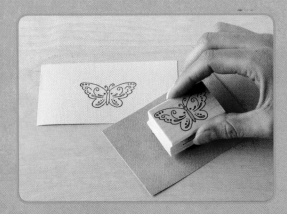

2 Cut around the perimeter of the entire image from one of the papers (light pink here). Then hand-cut just the body of the butterfly from the other paper (dark pink).

3 Adhere the butterfly body to the butterfly with foam tape. (Note: Foam tape can be cut to size if necessary.)

I wanted to give this page a sweet, vintage feel to go with the pictures of my grandpa and me. The floral paper I used for my accents was actually quite bright, so to give them a weathered look, I simply punched out flowers from the paper, applied glitter spray and crumpled them. By mounting them atop tissue-paper circles and finishing with a brad and rhinestone center, I produced aged, one-of-a-kind embellishments.

Hold On *by Elizabeth Kartchner.* **Supplies** *Cardstock:* Bazzill Basics Paper; *Patterned paper:* American Crafts (flowers), Jenni Bowlin Studio (tan) and SEI (blue dot); *Transparency:* Hambly Screen Prints; *Rub-on:* October Afternoon; *Rhinestones:* Glitz Design; *Letters, brads and pen:* American Crafts; *Chipboard and spray ink:* Tattered Angels; *Other:* Tissue paper, bingo card and tag.

43 Sew on your page in an innovative way.

Now, I know that some of you are a little intimidated by the thought of sewing on your layouts. I was at first, too, but now it's one of my go-to techniques. I just love that homespun effect and the versatility of adding my own personal touch to my pages. So even if you hand-stitch, it's time to play with needle and thread.

It's subtle, but look closely. Yep, Kelly stitched around the boy and the bucket in her photograph. It really helps her huggable little subject stand out from the background. You might want to practice a little first to get comfortable, but don't be scared. Look at the payoff!

Little Boy by Kelly Purkey. **Photo** by Susan Weinroth. **Supplies** *Cardstock, brad and pen:* American Crafts; *Patterned paper:* Denise Lynn Studios (elephants) and Heidi Grace Designs (orange and peach); *Stamp:* Hero Arts; *Ink and clip:* Stampin' Up!; *Letters:* Heidi Grace Designs; *Punches:* Fiskars Americas; *Other:* Thread.

You can actually sew through many more materials than you might think, even acrylic. For this project, I sewed fabric directly to an album. In addition to creating a nice look, sewing allowed me to create hidden pockets throughout my album. I simply stitched fabric onto cardstock, cut a strip for journaling, sewed along the edge and adhered it to the page. This little book contains photos I inserted throughout a year and journaling about moments where I felt I had grown or learned something.

"Learn & Grow" Album *by Elizabeth Kartchner.* **Supplies** *Album:* Rusty Pickle; *Cardstock and letters:* American Crafts; *Rub-ons, fabric strips and tag die cuts:* K&Company; *Buttons, pin and metal tabs:* Making Memories; *Adhesive:* Glue Dots International and Scrapbook Adhesives by 3L; *Other:* Thread and fabric remnants.

change happens
or a natural part

laughter is a

44 Take transparencies to a new level.

Sometimes we can get stuck in a rut with the ways we use our supplies. But if we can get beyond "This is used for this" thinking—oh, the possibilities! Try envisioning a new usage for a transparency to create a page that's clearly cool.

SWeeT
slumber

There are a million little things I could be doing right now
but here I am watching you sleep. i guess you could say that I
just can't get enough of you! you are precious!

I'm so glad I took on this challenge because I'm really pleased with how this page came out! The little glitter-filled transparency stars add such sweetness to these photos. To achieve the gentle lighting in these pictures, put your child to sleep by a window so the light casts soft shadows on your precious subject.

Sweet Slumber by Elizabeth Kartchner. **Supplies** *Patterned paper:* BasicGrey (birds), Creative Imaginations (scallop), Making Memories (blue) and Prima (purple); *Letters:* American Crafts; *Mini letters and glitter:* Making Memories; *Font:* CK Ali's Handwriting; *Adhesive:* Glue Dots International and Scrapbook Adhesives by 3L; *Other:* Transparency and thread.

Try this:

CREATE GLITTER PILLOWS

Mimic my technique to make sparkly cushions of any shape for your next project. It's really easy!

1. Punch a shape from a transparency. Use adhesive to position it where you'd like it on your layout. Machine-stitch the transparency directly to your page, leaving one corner open.

2. Carefully pour glitter inside the transparency shape you have sewn down.

3. Stitch the open corner closed to seal the pillow to your layout.

You can't help but "absolutely love" what Keisha did on this page—she created stamped layers on her layout using two sheets of transparencies. What a great way to add depth to a design. Try it!

Absolutely Loved *by Keisha Campbell.* **Supplies** *Cardstock:* Bazzill Basics Paper; *Patterned paper:* Collage Press; *Flower, ribbon and photo corners:* Making Memories; *Stamps:* Hero Arts and Stampin' Up!; *Tag and butterflies:* Martha Stewart for EK Success; *Other:* Rhinestones, file tabs, fonts, scallop punch and transparencies.

44 Get yourself inked.

No, I'm not suggesting you head out to the tattoo parlor. Instead, grab some ink and see where your imagination takes you. Sure, you may stain your fingers, but the permanently cool result on your pages is so worth a few temporary ink stains!

Since she uses ink on her layouts fairly regularly, Shelley challenged herself to apply it in as many ways as possible without overwhelming the page. She experimented with different surfaces—metals, transparencies, glass, fabric, etc.—but found that super-absorbent paper yielded her favorite result, the patina-like finish on the sides of the carousel. The star embellishments are actually the product of layering three different techniques. You may not feel as adventurous as Shelley, but take a cue from her and experiment with ink on your next page.

Round and Round on the Carousel by Shelley Aldrich. **Supplies**
Cardstock: EK Success; *Patterned paper:* Sassafras; *Chipboard:* Maya Road (wing) and Scenic Route (star); *Paint:* Ranger Industries; *Glitter:* EK Success; *Transparency:* 3M; *Ink:* Clearsnap (black); Ranger Industries (green and crackle); Glimmer Mist (spray ink), Tattered Angels; StazOn, Tsukineko; *Paint:* Liquitex; *Embroidery floss:* DMC; *Border punch:* Fiskars Americas; *Scalloped circle shape:* Sizzix, Provo Craft; *Colored pencils:* Prismacolor, Newell Rubbermaid; *Pen:* Zig Writer, EK Success.

I'm really into spray ink these days. You may have noticed it on a lot of my pages, because it's easy to use and allows me to add my personal touch. For this layout, I played with several colors of spray ink to create the tissue-paper flowers. I'll bet you'll have a ball with it—give it a whirl!

Always by Elizabeth Kartchner. **Supplies** *Cardstock:* Bazzill Basics Paper; *Patterned paper:* Sassafras and SEI; *Letters and rub-ons:* American Crafts; *Transparency:* Hambly Screen Prints; *Spray ink:* Glimmer Mist, Tattered Angels; *Buttons:* Making Memories; *Font:* 2Peas Sailboat; *Adhesive:* Glue Dots International and Scrapbook Adhesives by 3L; *Other:* Thread and tissue paper.

Try this:

FORM BLOSSOMS FROM TISSUE PAPER

These delicate flowers add a charming, old-fashioned feeling to any page. Follow the simple instructions to whip up a few today!

1 To make two sizes of circles, trace onto layers of tissue paper using the bottoms of different-sized cups. (Note: The tissue paper can be plain or patterned.) Spray the tissue-paper circles with spray ink and let dry.

2 Crumple and wrinkle the tissue-paper edges.

3 Layer the circles and finish with a button center.

46 Embrace a sticky situation.

Glue isn't just an adhesive; it can help you produce some really incredible effects. Combine glue with another medium and see what you come up with. You may find yourself stuck on the results—in a good way!

Sasha's approach to this challenge isn't complicated in the least. She simply drew circles with her glue pen and added some glitter to them. Don't worry about perfection—the loopy doodles will add oodles of charm to your page.

Angels, Ours *by Sasha Farina.* **Supplies** *Cardstock:* Bazzill Basics Paper (blue, green and red) and KI Memories (lace); *Patterned paper:* Collage Press (red floral), GCD Studios (red grid), Making Memories (blue leaf), Sassafras (text) and Scenic Route (lined); *Flowers:* Prima; *Chipboard accents:* Fancy Pants Designs; *Rub-ons:* Hambly Screen Prints; *Stickers:* 7gypsies (sentiment) and October Afternoon (letters); *Spray glitter:* Tattered Angels; *Glitter:* Making Memories; *Gloss medium:* Ranger Industries; *Adhesive:* Zig 2-Way Glue, EK Success; *Other:* Buttons, rickrack, corner-rounder punch and thread.

Have you ever stamped with a glue pad? Instead of transferring ink onto your project, you'll have a sticky image. For this challenge, I sprinkled flocking on the gluey stamped surface (see the blue swirl?), but glitter or tiny beads would work equally well. Try it for yourself!

Any Day Now *by Elizabeth Kartchner.* **Supplies** *Patterned paper:* BasicGrey (brown), Prima (blue dot) and Sassafras (scalloped); *Letters:* BasicGrey; *Ruler:* September 2008 Kit of the Month; *Stamp:* Fancy Pants Designs; *Ink:* Tsukineko; *Flocking:* Doodlebug Design; *Clouds:* Sprinkles Brushes by Tia Bennett; *Software:* Adobe Photoshop CS2; *Font:* 2Peas Tubby: *Other:* Thread, buttons, glue pad and flowers.

Quiz:

Are you a technique geek?

I realize that not everyone is technique-y. There are definite levels of "geekdom" in this area. Just where do you fall on the continuum?

Scoring: Count up the checks and circles, and add them together.

0–15: You may have just started scrapbooking, or you may scrap digitally, or you may like to keep it simple. No worries! Do what pleases you, but don't be afraid to step outside your comfort zone, either.

15–30: You may own a decent amount of tools and mediums, but you may not use them very frequently. You may not consider techniques your strong suit. Let the challenges in this chapter stretch you, and you just might add some new tricks to your scrapbooking repertoire.

30–45: You're well-supplied and have attempted a good variety of techniques. I bet you're already rarin' to get started on this chapter's challenges, so get to it!

46-60: You're a technique geek. You love playing and getting messy and are practically fearless about learning new things. I could probably learn a lot from you. Go on with your bad self!

How many of the following supplies do you have in your stash?
Place a checkmark next to all that apply.

How many do you actually use with some regularity?
Circle all that apply.

○ Alcohol ink	○ Hot-glue gun
○ Binding system	○ Iron
○ Bone folder	○ Light box
○ Brayer	○ Needle
○ Chalk	○ Notch tool
○ Circle cutter	○ Paint
○ Craft knife	○ Paper piercer
○ Crimper	○ Punches
○ Die-cut tool or machine	○ Rub-on tool
○ Distressing ink	○ Sander or edge distresser
○ Embossing powder	○ Sewing machine
○ Eyelet setter	○ Stamping ink
○ Grommet tool	○ Stamps
○ Hammer	○ Stapler
○ Heat tool	○ Tag maker

LIZZY'S LAST WORD:

Tech(nique) savvy

I would fully qualify as a technique geek. I'm constantly evolving and learning—it's a big part of what makes scrapbooking so fun for me. Here's a little peek inside my craftiness:

CK: What have been some of your go-to techniques through the years?

EK: I've always been excited to come up with cool, new uses for scrapbooking supplies, and I like to push myself to design and journal inventively, too, which often involves trying a fresh technique. Other constants for me include striving to keep balance on my pages and coordinating fun, bright colors.

CK: Have your technique preferences changed over time?

EK: Yes, I incorporate more techniques now. I've always tried lots of different things, but maybe I'm a bit braver these days.

CK: What are some of your current favorite techniques?

EK: I'm really into sewing on my pages, using spray ink and spray glitter, and coming up with new ways to display my journaling.

CK: How do you learn new techniques?

EK: It's really all about inspiration. I'm constantly browsing online, seeing what catches my eye—from clothing details at online retailers to color combinations on home-decor blogs to cool layout ideas from online scrapbooking galleries. Then I just try to think of how I could incorporate what I've seen onto my own pages. Many original techniques have developed in that very way!

CK: Why do you think it's important for scrapbookers to try new techniques?

EK: Because it pushes you and keeps the hobby fun and exciting. When you attempt new things, you're trying on different styles, and that's how you discover your authentic scrapbooking style.

photo fun

Stripped down to its barest element, scrapbooking is the art of the photo. Now, you know I love journaling, techniques and products! But the photos are the stars of the page, period. Let's focus on taking and using photos for the challenges in this chapter.

47 Highlight—don't hide—an imperfect shot.

We've all got them—blurry, dark, poorly composed, finger-in-the-corner "duds" in our photo stacks. But sometimes, despite the less-than-stellar quality, these pictures just somehow have special meaning to us. I challenge you to embrace a flawed gem and make it work!

Collin and I had set the timer for this picture, but the focus wasn't quite right. Yet, of all the shots from that day, I couldn't stop looking at this one. It had such a soft tenderness I couldn't resist. Using "rough"-looking supplies like cardboard and masking tape and an antique typewriter font helped me echo the mood of the photo and document the things I cherish about our relationship.

My Heart Tells Me by Elizabeth Kartchner. **Supplies** *Cardstock:* Bazzill Basics Paper; *Patterned paper:* Rusty Pickle; *Rub-ons and transparency:* Hambly Screen Prints; *Adhesive badge:* American Crafts; *Letter stickers and heart rub-ons:* Making Memories; *Stamps:* Studio G; *Ink:* StazOn, Tsukineko; *Text tape:* Prima; *Dot mask:* Heidi Swapp for Advantus; *Font:* American Typewriter; *Adhesive:* Glue Dots International and Scrapbook Adhesives by 3L; *Other:* Cardboard, masking tape, pen and paint.

Whenever you're photographing active kids, you're going to end up with shots like these. Beth's focal-point photo was blurry and had some distracting background elements, but she loved her little subject's expression. And the bottom photo was out of focus because she was being tickled. In both cases, Beth camouflaged the flaws by layering other elements on top, such as the title, the photo corner and even another photo. The use of multiple photos gives the eye lots to look at so it doesn't dwell on the imperfection of the photography.

Little Miss Personality by Beth Opel.
Supplies *Cardstock:* Bazzill Basics Paper; *Patterned paper:* Making Memories; *Letter stickers:* American Crafts ("Miss"), BasicGrey ("Little") and Paislee Press ("Personality"); *Flower transparency:* Hambly Screen Prints; *Rhinestones:* Heidi Swapp for Advantus; *Scallop-edge frame:* My Mind's Eye; *Paper borders:* Doodlebug Design; *Bird accent and pen:* American Crafts; *Font:* Beau; *Other:* Chipboard photo corner.

At the Patch by Kelly Purkey. **Supplies** *Cardstock and pen:* American Crafts; *Patterned paper:* American Crafts (green stripe) and Heidi Grace Designs (orange); *Transparency:* Hambly Screen Prints; *Stamps and rhinestones:* Hero Arts; *Ink:* Stampin' Up!; *Chipboard:* Heidi Grace Designs; *Punches:* Fiskars Americas.

48 Write or stamp directly on a photo.

Try using the photo itself as a canvas for your creativity. Make sure the photo you select is not an original—print a duplicate so the real one is intact, but have a ball writing, doodling or stamping right on your picture.

Photos with big, blue skies are perfect for journaling on. You're not covering up anything too important in the photo, and the color still comes through nicely. Follow Kelly's lead and write your journaling in an open space on one of your pictures. (*Note:* Make sure to choose a pen that is made for writing on photos.)

By placing my photos so there was room to the right, I had just enough space to give Quincey a pair of stamped wings. For the best results when stamping on a photo, make sure to use ink that's designed for slick surfaces. If you like, add glitter for a little extra sparkle.

She Traded in Her Wings by Elizabeth Kartchner. **Supplies** *Cardstock:* Bazzill Basics Paper; *Patterned paper:* My Mind's Eye (blue) and Sassafras (decorative-edged); *Transparency:* Hambly Screen Prints; *Letters, adhesive badge and pen:* American Crafts; *Journaling spot, arrow and clip:* Making Memories; *Rhinestones:* Glitz; *Ticket:* Jenni Bowlin Studio; *Stamp:* Hot Off The Press; *Ink:* StazOn, Tsukineko; *Ribbon:* SEI; *Glitter:* Ranger Industries; *Other:* Tag, glitter and scalloped circle punch.

49 Use old photos of people at the same age.

You're going to love this one! Pull out old prom shots of you and your friends, or baby photos of each of your children, or Little League pictures of both of your brothers, or any photos of people at similar stages in their lives, and create a layout about them. Get ready for a trip down memory lane!

Cindy's layout just makes me smile! She used photos of both her husband and herself when they were about three months old as a springboard for a layout documenting the history of their relationship. The sweet colors and accent choices bridge the gap from infancy to love story. Adorable!

Little Did They Know by Cindy Tobey. **Supplies** Cardstock: Bazzill Basics Paper; Patterned paper: Fancy Pants Designs (blue) and Making Memories (pink dot); Ribbon: Cosmo Cricket (blue scalloped) and Michaels (brown stripe); Felt: American Crafts (hearts) and Fancy Pants Designs (scalloped border); Clip and chipboard: Making Memories; Adhesive badge: American Crafts; Button and acrylic heart: Fancy Pants Designs; Letters: Scenic Route; Font: Courier New; Other: Thread and corner-rounder punch.

Looks like Cindy and I were on the same wavelength for this one! While she focused on where the future would take her and her husband, however, I used the photos of Collin and me from grade school to contrast our personalities at the time. Yep, the spelling bee champ married the class clown, and life has never been more delightful. A little journaling tucked behind the photos tells the story more thoroughly.

School Days by Elizabeth Kartchner. **Supplies** *Patterned paper:* Bam Pop (lockers), BasicGrey (brown) and Scenic Route (lined); *Letters:* American Crafts (title) and Jenni Bowlin Studio ("notes"); *Foam accent and pen:* American Crafts; *Buttons:* Sassafras; *Frame die cuts:* Bam Pop; *Journaling card:* Kit of the Month; *Adhesive:* Scrapbook Adhesives by 3L and Mini Glue Dots, Glue Dots International; *Other:* Paper clip and thread.

50 Arrange your photos in a visual triangle.

Remember back on p. 65 when I talked about the visual triangle? Three is a powerful design number, so for this challenge, organize your layout so the photos provide a triangular road map for the eye. If you're up to it, use the visual triangle for other elements on your page as well. On the count of three . . . go!

Examining Kelly's layout with this challenge in mind, we can clearly see the visual triangle at work. Placing her photos in this arrangement gives her page a nice flow and balance. She further harnessed the power of three with the trio of similarly sized circles and the three sections of orange dot paper.

Continental *by Kelly Purkey.* **Supplies** *Cardstock, pen and brads:* American Crafts; *Patterned paper:* Heidi Grace Designs; *Die-cut machine and mini letter stickers:* Making Memories; *Stamps and ink:* Stampin' Up!; *Epoxy stickers:* Cloud 9 Design; *Buttons:* 7gypsies; *Circle cutter, punches and adhesive:* Fiskars Americas; *Other:* Thread.

Someday I hope you will think it is cool that your mommy can peel an orange in one long strip. Because I remember when my dad would do it and I thought it was the coolest thing ever! I am sure you will someday...but for now we will just enjoy one of our favorite afternoon snacks.

My visual triangle may not be as apparent, but look closely. There are three small circular photos on the bottom half of the layout that create their own mini triangle. But beyond that, consider that the three of them, along with the other circular elements, work together as one third of a triangle that travels from the top-left photo to the top-right photo down to the cluster below. It's subtle, but it leads the eye to all of the components that make the layout work.

Cool Mom Skill by Elizabeth Kartchner. **Supplies** Cardstock: Wausau Paper; Patterned paper: American Crafts and Doodlebug Design; Letters: BasicGrey; Dimensional stickers: KI Memories; Chipboard arrow: American Crafts; Paper border: Doodlebug Design; Button: Autumn Leaves; Font: 2Peas Sailboat; Adhesive: Glue Dots International and Scrapbook Adhesives by 3L; Other: Circle punches.

51 Make a photo the base of your layout.

The key to this challenge is choosing a picture that has a lot of open space so you can add stuff on top of it. If you don't have a photo printer that allows you to make a large enough print, order a picture from your local photo lab. Backing your layout with a big picture makes a big impact!

I can't get enough of this adorable shot of Avery's little beach body. Notice how the angle helps direct attention into the layout. Before I sent my picture to the lab, I cropped it into a square to work as the base for my 12" x 12" page, and added journaling directly to the photo. To achieve the swirled text, I simply typed it out in Photoshop, highlighted each sentence and clicked on Warp Text to shape them into waves. This layout is a great memory of a happy day!

A Day in the Sun by Elizabeth Kartchner. **Supplies** *Patterned paper and flower:* Sassafras; *Transparency:* Hambly Screen Prints; *Houndstooth sticker and bird accent:* American Crafts; *Rub-ons:* K&Company; *Metal tag:* Pebbles Inc.; *Font:* AL Evening Stroll; *Adhesive:* Glue Dots International; Scrapbook Adhesives by 3L; *Other:* Ribbon, word die cut and sequins.

Amanda practiced her spray-painting technique before actually applying it to her big photo. She cut cardstock shapes, mounted them onto the background using rubber cement and sprayed the paint. When it was dry, she just rubbed off the rubber cement! Her title adds a spot of color—she hand-cut it from patterned paper—and the perfect finishing touch to this funky page.

I Adore Being a Girl by Amanda Johnson.
Supplies *Patterned paper:* Hambly Screen Prints; *Label-maker:* Dymo; *Pen:* Uni-ball Signo, Newell Rubbermaid; *Other:* Paint, cardstock (for stencil) and thread.

52 Take photos of a collection.

You've got the collection, or your husband does, or maybe it's your child's.
Honor the time spent amassing the collection by photographing and creating
a page about it. It's a piece of your life that needs to be remembered!

I'll bet you have a collection of happy scrappy stuff like Sasha's! I love how she took photos from several different angles to make it more interesting. Why not create a page about the goodies that make up your scrap stash?

Colors *by Sasha Farina.* **Supplies** *Cardstock:* Bazzill Basics Paper; *Patterned paper:* Hambly Screen Prints (grid) and Scenic Route (white outline); *Rub-ons and transparencies:* Hambly Screen Prints; *Stickers:* Creative Imaginations (phrase), Doodlebug Design (blue letters) and Pink Paislee (yellow letters); *Stamps:* Autumn Leaves (frame) and FontWerks (circles); *Ink:* VersaFine, Tsukineko; *Pen:* Uni-ball, Newell Rubbermaid; *Other:* Buttons and "love" sticker.

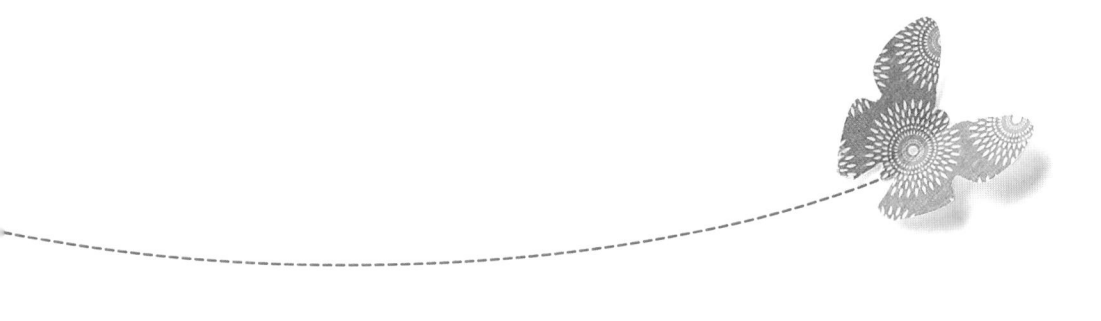

Oh, taking the photos for this layout was such a neat experience for me! I merely followed Avery around all day and snapped shots of her playing with her collection of toys. I really got an accurate glimpse of her status as the Queen of Toyland, and so I crowned her right on the page.

Queen of Toyland by Elizabeth Kartchner. **Supplies** Cardstock: Bazzill Basics Paper; Patterned paper: American Crafts and KI Memories; Chipboard, adhesive badge, rub-ons and pen: American Crafts; Flower: Sassafras; Button: KI Memories; Font: Little Days; Adhesive: Glue Dots International and Scrapbook Adhesives by 3L; Other: Rhinestones and punches.

Quiz:

What's your focus?

Write your answers on the blanks provided, then check below to see if there are any takeaway tips you can add to your skill set.

Answers:

1. Remove distracting elements. In this case, clear off the table. Before you get ready to take any photo, look at it through the camera's viewfinder and eliminate anything extraneous.

2. Shoot from above. For some reason, most people look best when the camera is positioned above them. When they're looking up, there's less chance of the dreaded double-chin effect.

3. Turn off the flash. Indirect sunlight is by far the most pleasing light, so place your subjects near a window for some beautifully lit photos.

4. Get closer. Your subjects will be so engaged in their fun that they'll hardly notice you. Even if they pose, their interaction will provide some memorable shots. This is probably my number-one piece of advice for better photos!

5. Take lots of photos. The more pictures you take, the greater your odds of getting a good one. It's as simple as that!

1 You're sitting around the table after a meal, and someone decides you need a photo to remember the occasion. Before you all pose, what needs to be done?

_____

_____

_____

2 You want to take some flattering portrait shots of your mom or sister. Where should you position yourself in relationship to your subject to get the most complimentary pictures?

_____

_____

_____

3 You're inside with your family on a cold but sunny afternoon. If you want to photograph your loved ones, what simple adjustment should you make to your camera?

_____

_____

_____

4 You're on a bench at the playground enjoying the giggles and grins of your daughter and her playmates. You want to capture their infectious happiness. What should your first move be?

_____

_____

_____

5 You're at a wedding, and the bridal party is posed for a group shot. What should you do to up your odds of getting a photo where everyone looks good?

_____

_____

_____

LIZZY'S
LAST WORD:
Picture pointers

Over the years I've developed some tried-and-true camera techniques. Feel free to benefit from these tips!

FUN PHOTO-OPS

- Stuff you do every day (someday you'll cherish these shots)

- Laughing or being silly (capturing personalities is so fun)

- Sleeping babies (there's nothing sweeter)

- Timer shots (get in the picture already!)

- Shots from above or below (nab those cool angles)

EDITING FAVES

- Desaturating a bit of the reds in a photo, then upping the contrast for a cool vintage look

- Actions by Maggie Holmes (MaggieHolmes.Typepad.com)

- Totally Rad Actions (GetTotallyRad.com)

- MiaBella Actions (LeahProfancik.com)

PHOTO STORAGE

- On my computer in folders titled with the month and year

- In files within each folder organized by key words

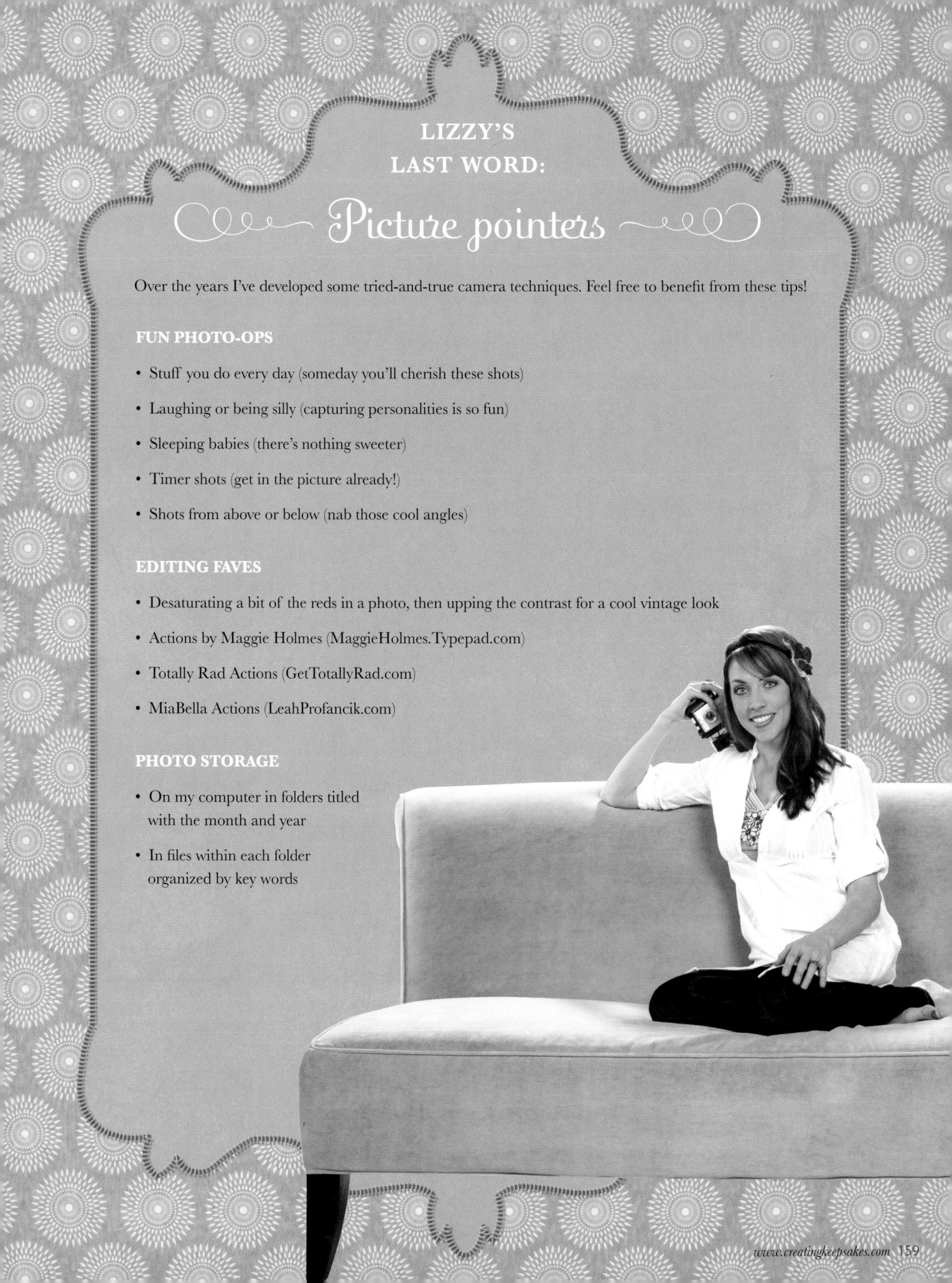

Contributors

Meet the talented team of Scrapbookers who took up the challenge and learn about the fun connections between them.

Backgrounds and butterflies throughout this book were created from papers by: BasicGrey, BoBunny Press, Crate Paper, Dream Street Papers, K&Company, My Mind's Eye, Pebbles Inc., Sassafrass, Scenic Route and We R Memory Keepers.

Paper flowers shown on pages 44-45 were made by Julie Wilson at prettylittleflowers1.blogspot.com.

Amanda Johnson
North Canton, OH
candimandi.typepad.com

Amanda and Keisha are both on the 2009 Jenni Bowlin Design Team.

Beth Opel
Saratoga Springs, UT
bethandsusanopel.typepad.com

Beth was Keisha's high school English teacher. Elizabeth and Beth have the same given name.

Kelly Purkey
Brooklyn, NY
kellypurkey.typepad.com

Kelly, Cindy and Mou are all 2009 Creating Keepsakes Dream Team members.

Mou Saha
Tampa, FL
collagecollagecollage.blogspot.com

Mou and Beth were both Creating Keepsakes Scrapbooker of the Year finalists in 2006.

Cindy Tobey
Kentwood, MI

cindytobey.blogspot.com

Cindy and Kelly both grew up near Grand Rapids, Michigan.

Elizabeth Kartchner
Pleasant Grove, UT

elizabethkartchner.blogspot.com

Elizabeth, Keisha and Sasha each have two daughters.

Keisha Campbell
Leesburg, VA

abiteast.typepad.com

Four contributors have Asian connections: Keisha recently moved back from China, Sasha lives in Singapore, Kelly was born in Korea and Mou is originally from India.

Sasha Farina
Singapore

shopaholicscrapper.blogspot.com

Sasha and Amanda are both on the 2009 Hambly Design Team.

Shelley Aldrich
Rancho Palos Verdes, CA

shelleyaldrich.blogspot.com

Shelley and Mou were both Creating Keepsakes *Scrapbooker of the Year finalists in 2008.*

Sheri Reguly
Thunder Bay, ON, Canada

Sheri, Cindy and Mou each have one son and one daughter. Sheri and Mou were both Creating Keepsakes *Hall of Famers in 2007.*

Take up the challenge

Here's your chance to set forth a "plan of attack" for putting what you've learned to use.

Thanks for joining me on this creative adventure!

♡ lizzy

What challenges are calling your name? Write them down. Of course, if your answer is "All of Them," I won't be upset at all!

_____

_____

_____

Which of the "Try This" techniques are you itching to attempt? Write down the techniques here.

_____

_____

_____

Are there any page designs you just have to scraplift? List the titles below.

_____

_____

_____

Did any layout topics inspire you? What were they?

_____

_____

_____

Do you have any goals for your scrapbooking? If so (and I hope you do!), record them here.

_____

_____

_____

Finally, use the lines below to list the reasons you scrapbook. Refer back often so you never forget.

_____

_____

_____